The Alignment Focused Life

"Your guide to healthy relationships, wellness and prosperity"

The Alignment Focused Life

"Your guide to healthy relationships, wellness and prosperity"

Brian Schneider, PhD

ISBN: 978-1-956074-25-3 (Paperback Edition)
ISBN: 978-1-956074-26-0 (Hardcover Edition)
ISBN: 978-1-956074-24-6 (E-book Edition)

Book Ordering Information

Phone Number: 315 288-7939 ext. 1000 or 347-901-4920
Email: info@globalsummithouse.com
Global Summit House
www.globalsummithouse.com

Printed in the United State of America

Table of Contents

Chapter 1 – The Importance of Alignment

In my 30 years of practice, I recognized that most of my clients we're not in alignment with their values and goals. They were basically living unfocused lives and hoping for a miracle. YOU MUST BE THE MIRACLE. This book is focused on all the elements that can go wrong in your life, probably have gone wrong, and how your life can change dramatically once you are focused and in healthy alignment.

Why is alignment important? Alignment is the key to healthy relationships, wellness, prosperity and financial health. Let me give you 2 examples of how alignment works. The first example is the military. In this organization, millions of people come from all over the country, go to basic training for a few months and then are prepared to survive and meet most challenges. How is this possible? I was in the military for almost 6 years and I can tell you that people in the military are from all walks of life. In the civilian world, these people would struggle to get along and would have difficulty producing the kind of results the military requires. The most amazing thing about the military is that it is comprised of primarily young boys and girls and they literally go around the world and put their lives on the line for people like you and me. They could never come together in such a short time to do this difficult task without extreme alignment. They are focused on a purpose and respect the fact that alignment is necessary, even critical, for success.

Alignment also occurs with dancing. You may not be able to dance well, and your partner may also not dance well, but if you can dance together and are in alignment with each other, then you will be successful. It's all about understanding each other and compensating so that both of you are in alignment and able to dance. The only thing that will matter is that you will both be satisfied with the result. Alignment breeds satisfaction and resolution.

Unfortunately, alignment today is primarily focused on NEXT and MORE. If a relationship goes south and when many people feel it's time to move on, NEXT – on to the next relationship, which will often provide the same drama or problems that exists with the current relationship. Sometimes a job is the focus of the NEXT syndrome. Rather than accepting mediocrity or learning to live with less, it is much easier to shout NEXT and move on to the next job, which is often no better than your current job. Many Americans today have a short fuse and short attention span. We get bored easily and we're always searching for the NEXT thing to make our lives better.

Another characteristic of life in America is the desire for MORE. In Japan, the average person saves about 25% of their income. In America, we are in the negative space. We don't save, we spend. We spend so much; we go into debt. The #1 reason for divorce in America is debt. It was also the most common problem I saw in practice. Americans are so focused on new cars, new houses, new clothes and new furniture, we forget how to balance our check books and inevitably fall into debt. We have an insatiable appetite for "things" and we love new stuff - especially when it's on sale. Unfortunately, MORE stuff, debt and stress has driven us to obesity, heart disease, divorce and bankruptcy. The alignment on NEXT and MORE has crippled America and prompted addiction which is often the only means of escape for many people. As an addiction's therapist, I can tell you there is an epidemic of drug and alcohol addiction in this country because we are overwhelmed and need an escape plan. NEXT and MORE are simply not the answer – alignment in relationships, health and finances is the only solution which requires assessing the needs, accepting the consequences and exercising the discipline necessary to attain focus and alignment.

Chapter 2 - You Will Attract What You Radiate

Misalignment frequently occurs in 3 key areas: relationships, health and finances. In the area of relationships, we often believe that love is a noun, meaning that love is a person, place or thing. We're looking for external answers to really solve an internal problem. This can lead to enormous conflict. You can spend an entire lifetime looking for that soul mate or perfect person to solve all of your problems and make you happy. You may seek a certain place that has warm weather or a big city that you think will solve your problems to make you happy. Many of us are stuck in the dream of winning the lottery and think lots of money will solve all of our problems. The truth is that most lottery winners are broke, divorced or searching for more within just 3 years after winning the lottery. I once worked with an NFL player who had won the lottery twice, lost everything on drugs and gambling and was speaking in the clinic I worked at to warn the clients about the dangers of gambling or thinking the lottery is the answer for all their problems.

Alignment is the key and this book will explain how easy it is to get out of alignment and the importance of knowing your goals, what's truly important and learning to focus and seek alignment even when the world is telling you different.

The permanent solution for healthy relationships is usually not external in the form of a noun, but love is a verb. Love is being considerate, humble or grateful then aligning with another person such as a young child, teenager, parent, boss, coworker or spouse for instance. Each alignment requires a different set of characteristics on your part. For instance, parenting a child requires setting good boundaries, understanding that most children are looking for attention and you must extinguish the behavior that's negative. You always want to catch your child doing something good, then reinforce it positively with attention. You never want to reinforce negative behavior with attention. When you use positive reinforcement, the negative behavior will often extinguish. As a parent, you want to model positive behavior. Modeling is a very important influence on children and by radiating positive behavior you will attract the kind of relationship you desire.

Finding the 'right person" is a tedious process that most of us have experienced more times than we care to admit. I can share with you some of my observations from doing couples therapy for 30 years. LOVE IS NOT TO BE FOUND BUT MADE. That is the simple truth I discovered from working with successful couples over the years. It is a process of accepting fault and surrendering to the fact that none of us are perfect. Focus on yourself and realize that LOVE IS A VERB - an action word. You must be humble, considerate and grateful before you align with anyone. Trust is the most important thing in any relationship and until you've surrendered your ego and can honestly admit the mistake, we've all made – "I was only thinking of myself" you will never be completely satisfied in a relationship. Humility sets you free.

If you have the opposite problem, a dependent personality for instance, healthy boundaries and assertiveness are the key to a successful relationship, or the benchmark that indicates it may be time to move on to a healthy relationship.

The primary problem for health typically is from the neck up. What I mean by that is that we simply want what tastes good, smells good, looks good and feels good. Unfortunately, this is the basis for most addictions. Many health problems start from the neck up. Addiction to drugs, alcohol and junk food is focused from the neck up and poor impulse control leads to chronic disease. In my practice, I used to have clients sit in a chair with a black sack over their head. I would say to the group, "Now let me see you practice addiction". Certainly, addiction is no longer a problem when you're focused from the neck down.

DEBT is a 4-letter word. America has become a nation of debtors. We are one of the worst savers in the world. Unfortunately, we are bombarded by advertising and the average American is now over $20,000 in debt not including a mortgage. There are countries in the world that save 25% of everything they earn, but in America we are in the negative balance. Unfortunately, because we have poor impulse control, we spend too much and we engage in activities that cause us to be addicts, such as junk food addiction, alcoholism and drug addiction. Poor impulse control and poor frustration tolerance are the seeds for many dysfunctional behaviors.

Healthy finances are a matter of maintaining a budget that you actually follow that reflects your income, staying out of debt when possible or at least paying it down as quickly as possible, learning to give or tithe and then ultimately learning how to invest. Unfortunately, for most of us debt is like a brick wall. It stops us from saving and especially investing. lexingtonlaw.com was one of my favorite websites I referred to my clients. It's a monthly service and they helped many of my clients reduce or even pay off their debt. Debt does not discriminate against anyone. I had very bright, very educated and very successful clients that were handcuffed by debt. Debt is often listed as the #1 reason for divorce. I had so many clients over the years that could just never get past the financial problems in their relationship and ultimately separated or divorced. The same couples who started in perfect alignment when they began, deteriorated after years of financial problems until everything was over.

Healthy relationships, wellness and prosperity are the results of focus on healthy alignment, assessing the problems, making the important decisions and accepting the magic 10 – 2 letter words, "IF IT IS TO BE IT IS UP TO ME"

Chapter 3 – My Journey

My journey began in 2008. It was the end of my life as I knew it. That year I endured everything from divorce and losing my family of 26 years, a stroke that put me into a 5-month coma, I lost my license to practice, I lost every cent I had worked for and I needed to lose 200 pounds. A rough day at the office.

Suddenly, nothing made sense and everything I had worked for was gone. It's a rude awakening for anyone to face poverty, obesity, joblessness and divorce within a short time. It's particularly difficult for someone who has just earned 3 college degrees and was referred to as "doctor" by people I respected. My plan wasn't working and I had no plan "B". Many years later, I reviewed and assessed the mess I was in and scaled my current alignment in 2017. I essentially gave my relationships, health and finances an F. The honor roll student with 3 degrees was suddenly last in his class and was being called down to the principal's office. I began to hear a Sergeant from my Air Force days whisper in my ear something he had said years ago, "You can't fertilize a 40 acre field with a fart." I actually began to understand what that meant and it basically summarized my current situation.

The next couple of years in my journey was an experience I will never forget. This was a time when "The Great Depression 2.0" was happening in America and a lot of people lost their homes or were in foreclosure. I actually had 2 different friends during this period in foreclosed homes that let me stay in their homes, rent free of course. My sweet mother died during this time and unexpectedly left me a little money which helped me buy a car from a buy here, pay here dealer. I had a very difficult time driving a car after a stroke and a 5-month coma and 4 accidents followed. When I told the buy here, pay here dealer I had just totaled his car in an accident, he called me names I hadn't even heard in the military. This was one time I was glad I was broke. The dealer couldn't sue me or as they say "You can't get blood from a turnip."

After a year of pleading, begging and writing many letters, I was finally able to get a Senator in Washington, then a Congressman, then a state commissioner and finally my request landed on the Governor's desk for approval. Even then, it took a friend at the VA to call the governor and send a letter and then suddenly, it appeared, a letter recertifying my license to practice. YIPPEEE!!!!!

In the year ahead, I had to take jobs I was overqualified for, but I'm not complaining. My journey was taking a turn in the road and I was headed to prosperity, but I learned the hard way that sometimes you have to lose yourself to find yourself. My precious ego had just been squashed and I was left on the side of the road to die. What I didn't know at the time, I was eating humble pie and thankful that I was at least eating something…...anything. It's hard to be humble. What I learned from my painful journey – REMEMBER THE BEST AND FORGET THE REST.

Chapter 4 – Defense Mechanisms

Offense is a whole lot more fun than defense. When you're on offense in football, you get to decide where you're going and the defense has to figure it out. As long as you can fool the defense, you'll always be ahead, but in life you are surrounded by snipers everywhere and the hardest part is we don't even know where they're hiding. Life is an obstacle course, a war for most of us and the enemy is winning. We have to wear so many hats....... parent, spouse, friend, co-worker, boss (sometimes a boss spelled backwards when your employees are a problem.... double SOB in case you didn't figure it out), teacher, student.... you get the idea. So many people are beat up by life, you crawl into a shrink's office (like mine) and say help, give me drugs and tell me everything's going to be alright. I would then listen to you talk for about 20 minutes often asking you many questions. A trade secret.... you can ask really tough questions to your clients and they won't get pissed off. At least they won' hit you or get physical (usually). Shrinks like to ask lots of questions, that's why we go to school half our lives. Once we assess your problems, then the wonderful diagnoses come. They are called DSM-V diagnoses and it's how we get paid. We must label you to get paid. Many times, I just wanted to say "this client is really messed up", but the depression, anxiety, etc. labels are inevitably the necessary choice.

Let's focus on the behaviors, thought patterns and personality styles that lead so many people into these diagnoses and out of alignment. We're so busy playing defense and navigating shark infested waters, we lose focus of our priorities, what's really important and then we spiral out of alignment and eventually find our way into the shrink's office. Most of these characteristics can be traced to childhood. One of the groups I did with my clients involved them (usually about 8 people) sitting in a semi-circle with one person just outside the circle and I would be right behind the client. The client would sit in three different chairs, one at a time, from right to left. The first chair was ages 2-12 and represented early childhood. The second chair in the middle-represented ages 13 – 18 (the adolescent years) and the final chair represented adulthood. The majority of my clients had the most difficult and painful emotions in the first two chairs. Childhood can be very painful and often abuse, trauma, abandonment, grief, separation and the seeds for depression, anxiety and addiction were planted and experienced during these years.

Personality disorders are pervasive and thought to be permanent. They are often a combination of a strong desire to be genuine or real but we also want to avoid conflict and tell everyone to give us space. Insight is the concept that we actually understand ourselves, but the problem with that is most people don't. The first step in gaining insight is to understand your personality. There are many different personality styles, but I'm going to focus on 2 personality styles that most people can relate to and have to understand to successfully function in a relationship.

Many males have a narcissistic personality. Not all males and some females are narcissistic. Narcissistic personality comes from the Greek God, Narcissus. He liked to look at his reflection in a pool of water. The Bible refers to this disorder as "selfish pride" and essentially the angel Lucifer was kicked out of heaven because he wanted to do what HE wanted to do WHEN he wanted to do it. I'm guessing a few females are reading this and saying "This sounds like my boyfriend or husband." Many first-born males are narcissistic and over 90% of US presidents and Fortune 500 CEOs are first born males. I am a first-born male but I am a "recovering" narcissist. My years as a selfish jerk are in the rear-view mirror precipitated by my wife who educated me by divorcing me. Education can be so expensive.

Another personality disorder that can lead to problems is dependent personality. This may cause "approval addiction" or difficulty setting strong boundaries and being assertive. Often times, the dependent personality may be passive and is taken for granted. They stay in unhealthy relationships and have trouble making decisions. If you are a dependent person, alignment is very difficult because the need for approval and the discomfort with confrontation is so pervasive.

Dependent personalities are often attracted to narcissistic personalities. Unfortunately, this relationship is either doomed or dysfunctional because love is a verb, an action word. To be successful, you must be humble, grateful and considerate but also be assertive with strong boundaries. There is nothing wrong with protecting you and frankly you have to be protective because there are so many challenges in the world and you have to protect yourself. By being assertive, humble, grateful and considerate and aligning with a person who respects you and you trust each other, a healthy relationship is very possible. Life is what happens when you're making plans, but when you are properly aligned and focused, it is so much easier to adjust and weather the difficult storms in life. Many males are basically microwaves and many women are crockpots. They are often not on the same page, but when they are aligned, meaning they negotiate, communicate assertively and are considerate of each other's needs, they can have a successful relationship.

Some of the characteristics we develop by adulthood that trigger defense mechanisms are narcissism, hedonism (pleasure obsession), inconsiderate, ungrateful, poor frustration tolerance (anger control), poor impulse control (addictions), undisciplined, feeling overwhelmed, loneliness, fear and attacks on self-esteem. Only the strong survive and if you want to thrive, you have to be aware of your personality, the issues that trigger your defense mechanisms and understand your priorities. When you have assessed these issues, then formulate a plan to reach satisfaction. We are all adjusting and we never cross the finish line or get everything we want. You must adjust and control what you can and accept what you can't. It really is a one day at a time battle.

10 Common Defense Mechanisms

It is common to repress, fabricate, blame someone else, rationalize, minimize or intellectualize and generally avoid responsibility as defense mechanisms are truly a passive approach that will short circuit problem solving and healthy confrontation. An assertive approach requires an appreciation for truth, honesty, genuine conversations and openness to understanding both sides of the issue. The following 10 defense mechanisms are common and can be a reason for poor communication that may lead to financial problems, parenting problems and ultimately divorce.

1. Sublimation
2. Projection
3. Compartmentalization
4. Denial
5. Intellectualization
6. Regression
7. Rationalization
8. Displacement
9. Repression
10. Lying

It is often difficult for couples to be assertive and constructive. Fear, anger, depression, anxiety, financial difficulties and unresolved issues can be road blocks for healthy communication and cause us to use defense mechanisms to protect ourselves. When you allow each other to be honest and remove fear, it is amazing how well you can communicate. Once you are back to being rational and assertive, review your priorities and goals.

Keep it simple, focus on one thing at a time and support each other. THERE'S NEVER A REASON TO BE DEFENSIVE WITH SOMEONE WHO YOU WOULD RATHER BE ON THE OFFENSE WITH.

Chapter 5 – Only Babies with Dirty Diapers Like Change

One of the first things every psychologist learns is that NO ONE likes change. Diets rarely work, only 10% of Americans exercise regularly and most Americans are in debt. We hate change or discomfort. We talk about it. I've had many clients spending a fortune to talk about it. People spend millions on diets and workout programs, but the problem is one simple thing: We don't have the discipline to change. We don't want to do what we don't want to do. I can give it a fancy label: poor frustration tolerance. Does that really help? Now you can tell everybody you have poor frustration tolerance. Only sweet little babies with dirty diapers like change.

One philosophy I respect is that we shouldn't give hungry fishermen fish, we should teach them how to fish. I always disliked seeing well intentioned people giving starving people in third world countries food, then wondering why those same people never got out of those tents or we're still hungry months or years later. Nothing was ever solved. It was a futile exercise, but hey they were doing good in the world. It never rang my bell because I always wanted to teach them how to fish, so to speak, so they could ultimately help themselves and then help someone else. The church I belong to does just that. They have sent over 60,000 members from the church to Rwanda to help this African nation that had basically imploded from a civil war in 1995. Today, Rwanda is considered the 2nd healthiest economy in Africa and Saddleback Church has been a big reason for this miraculous growth. I feel it's an investment and anyone can do well if they just get a chance and a little help.

Therapy can be just that. A little help. It's the process of learning how to fish. Too many doctors are prescribing a "pill for your ill" because it's easy to do, insurance companies pay for it and most patients are taking the poison (so to speak). For those that benefit from psychiatric medicine, good. But most people need therapy, or positive change, to affect any real, permanent change.

Happiness or being well adjusted, is often about establishing good habits. Most of us learn bad habits from an early age. Another doctor and I studied the psychological effects of a family eating a meal together once a day and actually talking to each other. We found there was an 80% improvement in communication and behavioral changes with the children. School performance got better and they actually learned problem solving skills and how to set good boundaries. The sad fact is that many families rarely have a meal together. Television, video games, the internet and cell phones have become baby sitters and a major source of entertainment. Microwave ovens and fast-food restaurants have replaced home cooked family dinners. This generation is labelled by many psychologists as the "entitlement" generation which is characterized by poor frustration tolerance and poor impulse control. An important consideration is that when the children become adults years later and someone like me gets them for therapy, that doctor will be addressing frustration tolerance, impulse control and coping skills and my company charged their insurance company $60,000 for one month of therapy known as Partial Hospitalization. Only babies with dirty diapers like change, but if you want to shape a healthy future, make the change NOW. Happiness is about making good choices and exercising the discipline to get it right. Could you imagine if I told a woman who learned she was pregnant that it won't hurt and don't focus on the sacrifice. Are you kidding me? It's gonna hurt so good! I have 2 kids and they are the best things that ever happened to me. Yes, the mother will have pain and there will be many sacrifices, but boy is it worth it.

The best things in life, pregnancy, a college degree, 30 years in a job with retirement, etc. are great, but challenging. You have to work and sacrifice for what you want and kids need to understand that. Embrace the sacrifice and accept it!

Chapter 6 – "I Guess You Need More Pain"

The drama and discoveries that occur in the privacy of a doctor's office doing therapy is incredible. The things people have told me over the years are mind blowing. I could hardly believe how some of my clients functioned in this world, but they did somehow. It's amazing what a person can do when they are unfocused and unaligned…. just drifting from paycheck to paycheck, relationship to relationship and job to job. Albert Einstein once said, "Insanity is the process of doing the same thing over and over expecting different results." Einstein never practiced psychology but he summed up my 30 years of practice in one sentence.

Individual therapy is the process of clients being heard, bitching about their problems, blaming everyone for the dysfunctional world they live in and expecting therapists like me to wave a magic wand. Only babies with dirty diapers like change, clients like to complain about life. Don't get me wrong. I loved my clients. For as difficult as they were, they were some of the most interesting people I've ever met. There is nothing quite like experiencing a breakthrough and witnessing real progress. There is nothing like it.

Individual therapy begins with assessment and then a diagnosis. I can't get paid until I hang a label on you. How do I assess you; you might ask? I complete, with you, a psychosocial which basically tells me your life story. What kind of student were you in school? Did you ever have any behavioral problems? What was your relationship like with your family? What were your favorite sports and hobbies? What were your favorite classes and what did you do best in? What's your history with sex and intimate relationships? Tell me about your work history. What's your greatest fear? What's your biggest accomplishment? I would want to know how well you've handled money. What's your work history? What's your history with friends? Have you ever been married…...any kids? What's your history with substance abuse? Do you have any mental health history? I would then ask you to scale your current self-esteem, impulse control, frustration tolerance and mood. By the way, most clients gave me 20 of 100 average for those 4 scales. Needless to say, you can see why they were in my office.

Individual therapy is assessing current function, determining current problems and then putting them on the board and developing a treatment plan. I always used Solution Focused Therapy and I would say, "You have told me that your average current score for self-esteem, frustration tolerance, impulse control and mood is 20 out of 100, what number would you like to be at by the time we finish therapy? The next question is absolutely crucial……What needs to happen so you can give me the number you want to be at? This becomes the basis for the treatment plan. Of course, the next step is the hardest. Are you willing to make changes so you can honestly give me higher scores? Now the real work begins.

Self-esteem begins with the important question. Why did you rate your self-esteem so poorly? Who told you that you are dysfunctional? You can almost always go back to their childhood and identify parents, teachers or authority figures such as coaches that ultimately trigger the client to believe they failed. Failure for a child can be devastating and have lifelong consequences. Dr. Karen Horney talked about the "tyranny of the shoulds." As children, we felt we never lived up to the shoulds and musts our parents and other authority figures set for us and as adults we "should and we "must" do things differently. Unfortunately, we get lost and then we "should all over ourselves" because we never lived up to their expectations. Dr. Albert Ellis stressed the importance of being rational and fair. He recommended not using words like always and never, because rarely is something always or never. It's not rational and leads to what's known as cognitive dissonance, or depression, anxiety or as many psychologists would say, "stinking thinking".

Self-esteem is improved by being rational and reasonable. The glass is half full, not half empty. YOU decide your self-esteem, not someone from your past or even your spouse or boss. You also have to ACCEPT what you cannot change and CHANGE what you can change. This is the Serenity Prayer. Focus and alignment will change dramatically when you practice these steps and evaluate your progress. YOU will be in charge of your life instead of your dysfunctional past.

The first question you have to ask regarding frustration tolerance is, what do you really need? It's been my experience that most people are overloaded and unfocused. I always go for finances first. Debt is the #1 reason for divorce and drives a lot of people into the shrink's office. I used lexingtonlaw.com as a service to help the client pay off debt and raise their credit score. I would ask the client, can you become a second-hand millionaire? I mean can you learn to buy stuff at thrift shops, Goodwill, e-bay? Basically, the client has to end their addiction to buying new stuff and focus on buying used stuff. You'd be amazed at how much you can save. I rarely buy anything new today because I can get such great deals if I just focus on saving money. Debt is often the main source for frustration tolerance problems and many people will self-medicate with addiction or casual sex to escape the pain. The alignment needs to be on prosperity which is reducing or retiring debt, sticking to a good budget and learning to save money, even if it's a small amount. You can make a lot of money if you start investing now and stick with it. The problem is people feel overwhelmed and never exercise the discipline to START SAVING TODAY!

Impulse control is the main behavioral problem and basis for most addictions. Saying no for many people is really difficult. I used to say to my clients, "I guess you need more pain." They wouldn't listen to me and heed my advice. They kept indulging in illegal drugs, unhealthy junk food, alcohol, promiscuous sex or illegal behavior. I was watching insanity, doing the same thing over and over, expecting different results, unfold before my eyes. At first, this was painful and very frustrating. I took it very personal, as do most therapists. I learned the old saying, "You can lead a horse to water, but you can't make him drink it." Sometimes, people need more pain and have to experience the situation themselves. Once they learn how to set boundaries and live within healthy boundaries, impulse control begins to improve.

Mood has both physical and mental causes but physical antecedents are often ignored or unrecognized. Stinking thinking or cognitive dissonance is the major culprit behind depression or anxiety. Depression typically focuses on prior unresolved events that still haunt the client and may cause self-blame. "Junk in the trunk" is unresolved baggage that needs to be addressed and resolved. Remember the serenity prayer……change what you can change and ACCEPT what you can't change. When there are unsolvable problems or unresolved issues, you just have to forgive and let go. There are many people who do not deserve to be forgiven, that's not the point. If you want to get better, you need to release the hurt. You're basically saying I can't handle this and I'm letting go. Forgiveness is healing and when you forgive, you will be set free from the pain. Sometimes it makes no sense and something as horrible as abuse may have happened to you, but by forgiving you begin to heal and are able to let go and move on with your life.

Financial problems may raise their ugly head resulting in depression or anxious mood. You've got to focus on spending less, staying in a healthy budget and reducing and eliminating debt should be a huge priority. I learned from 30 years in practice, debt is truly a 4-letter word and can upset your mood quicker than anything. Conversely, a debt free life can be very freeing and wonderful.

Relationships are uniquely human and kingdoms have been sacrificed and good people have been destroyed by them. We perceive love as a noun, meaning a person, place or thing. We think that love means finding our "soul mate" or that special person we can spend a lifetime with. Obviously, many people get divorced today so love really isn't a noun. The right alignment is that LOVE IS A VERB or action word. Love is being kind, considerate, grateful and humble then aligning with another person. Alignment with a child would have one set of characteristics but alignment with your spouse would have another set of characteristics. A committed relationship is built on trust, respect and communication. When I did couples therapy, I would ask them to scale trust, respect and communication from 0-100 and then discuss what was missing. Typically, what was needed was to ask the difficult questions and give each other permission to respond so neither person felt inhibited. Questions are powerful and when you feel free to speak your mind, progress is inevitable. Many couples have trouble communicating. Either one person is passive-aggressive (withholds information then becomes inappropriate) or aggressive meaning they want to dominate or control. The best solution is to be assertive. Say what you mean and mean what you say. Do it now, don't withhold. Good timing, a proper tone of voice and a constructive message will all lead to healthy assertive communication.

Individual therapy is a wonderful opportunity to get to know yourself and, more importantly, like yourself. When you can develop healthy frustration tolerance, impulse control, mood and self-esteem, your life will become much more manageable. Aligning with yourself and loving yourself is one of the most important things you can do.

Chapter 7 – "The Fountain of Youth"

What if I told you that there was an ancient "Fountain of Youth" that has been used by billions of people over thousands of years around the world? What if I told you that this "Fountain of Youth" received the Nobel Prize in 2016? What if I told you that a clinic in California has used this "Fountain of Youth" for over 30 years and were viewed as quacks 30 years ago, but are seen as geniuses today because the doctors that work there are submitting groundbreaking clinical research to the best medical journals in the world and proving how effective this "Fountain of Youth" is? What if I told you that many diseases and medical problems, such as cancer, diabetes, Alzheimer's, cardiovascular diseases and obesity, the main diseases Americans suffer from today, are actually being helped with this "Fountain of Youth". What if I told you that the Son of God who caused time to be divided into BC and AD went into a garden for 40 days and used this "Fountain of Youth" before he was killed on the cross.

I tried this "Fountain of Youth" several years ago and believed it to be a very bad idea and like most of the medical community, I vowed I wouldn't recommend it to anyone and I decided I would never try it again. I didn't get sick or have any real problems; I just didn't like it. I didn't believe it was healthy or a good idea. I was actually against it. Then it won a Nobel Prize in 2016 and several doctors, clinics and universities around the world began to use it and raved about it. Dr. Valter Longo from USC is on You Tube telling people how much your body loves this "Fountain of Youth." Jason Fung, MD has a You Tube channel telling people how great this is. Dr. Mindy Pelz has a Facebook group that actually meets and does it regularly. It has taken the medical community by storm and the results are undeniable.

Here is a list of what happens and proven when you engage in the "Fountain of Youth."

1. You will raise your growth hormone by 1300% in 12 hours.
2. You will raise ketones in 14 hours that will burn fat.
3. Autophagy will occur in 17 hours that will help you detoxify.
4. In 24 hours, your intestines and digestive system may be repaired.
5. Within 24 hours your body will start producing BDNF, which is brain food and will help with memory and mental acuteness.
6. Your blood pressure, blood sugar and inflammation levels may improve.
7. Within 36 hours you will lose body fat. You will lose approximately 1 pound per day.
8. You may increase stem cells, improve your immune system and repair injuries.
9. It is one of the healthiest things you can do.
10. The "Fountain of Youth" is better than many drugs or surgeries. It doesn't cost anything and will save you money. Weight loss, reduction in blood pressure, blood sugar and inflammation are possible. Every religion in the world uses it: Christianity, Judaism, Muslim, Buddhist, Hindu – all religions use it and view it as a holy practice. Billions of people around the world have used it and worship it. The scientific community shunned it as quackery until the Nobel Prize committee awarded a Japanese doctor in 2016 for his work on autophagy.

I tried this several years ago and didn't like it and swore I'd never do it again. Then after all the attention from the Nobel Prize and the buzz on the Internet with so many doctors and clinics using it, I thought I would try it again. This was in 2020 and I have to tell you it didn't go well the first few times. Finally, I got over the fear and read the science and I was hooked. I lost at least 1 pound per day, my energy went through the roof, my skin was shining and glowing and I looked and felt years younger. It was like a "spring cleaning" and I hadn't felt this good in years.

You must be patient when you begin this "Fountain of Youth", but when I watched patients in a clinic that had been practicing this for 35 years literally walk by the dining room (with food on the table) after several days of water fasting, I thought they should feel terrible or be starving, I was amazed and it gave me great confidence that I can do it and should do it.

Autophagy won the Nobel Prize in 2016 and that word means "self-eating" or fasting. Yes, fasting is a miracle "Fountain of Youth" that may help you lose weight, burn fat, repair injuries, reduce blood pressure, blood sugar and inflammation. Fasting repaired my brain which suffered a stroke and coma several years ago and repaired my right side that had been damaged by the stroke. I lost 200 pounds and I look and feel terrific. My picture is on my web site, discoverthealignmentfocusedlife.com.

If you just get through the first part, which I call the "Car Wash", fasting is a cleansing process and you will probably experience weakness and be tired until you get used to it. It's always a good idea to have a functional medical doctor check you out and even monitor your progress. A test called the A1C, very familiar to diabetics, is a good test to take and you want to obtain a score of 7.0 or below. You really should stop eating sugar and starch, which is a contributor for most diseases (obesity, heart disease, diabetes, cancer and Alzheimer's). There is a program called, "Forty Foods for Fitness" in this book and on my web site. The foods recommended will help you lower blood sugar. You want to eat foods that are 60 or below on the Glycemic Index.

Fasting is an excellent way to start a nutritional program because you will detox and it helps with weight loss. It will help increase discipline and change your attitude about food. Americans eat too much - especially unhealthy junk food. You can save money and you will look and feel better. Just watch the You Tube videos of Dr. Mindy Pelz, Dr. Jason Fung and True North Fasting Clinic in California on fasting or autophagy and they will be very helpful. Ask yourself why would the Son of God, who divided time (BC and AD), raised people from the dead, was resurrected himself and could do anything he wanted to do, but fasted his last 40 days on earth before he was crucified? Why did it win the Nobel Prize in 2016? Why do billions of people from every religion in the world practice fasting and view it as a holy practice? Maybe there's something to this.

Chapter 8 – The Body is a Temple

It may seem odd that a therapist like me would focus on physical problems since my training was in mental health, but about half way into my 30-year practice, I began to quickly realize that my clients were not physically well; they were toxic and had very poor energy, concentration and sleep habits. No wonder their lives were such a mess. The honest reality was that I too was a mess. I was a phony, talking the good talk and citing research for nutrition, yet never practicing what I preached. I was becoming worse than my clients until I finally became 200 pounds overweight, had a hemorrhagic stroke that nearly killed me and was in a coma for 5 months. I lost everything: my wife, my license to practice, my money, my house, my health and my mind. When I woke up from the coma, the last thing I remember was riding around in nature on my cross-country motorcycle. I felt free.

When I finally began to view food as fuel and my body as a temple and realized that we are so bombarded by advertising, restaurants and junk food, I accepted that we are in a war. Food manufacturers hide unhealthy ingredients, restaurants will sell junk food they obliterate for a few bucks. No one wants to cook anymore and sadly, many of us have no idea how to prepare meals. Even shopping in a grocery store can be an experience. I have taken many clients to the grocery store to teach them what I have learned. They are shocked at how much money they can save and how easy it is to improve their nutrition.

One of the most important things I stress is that most of us are focused from the neck up, meaning we want what will satisfy our taste, smell, sight and feelings more than anything. This is the foundation for addiction and why we have such problems with impulse control. When we begin to focus from the neck down, we support our liver, which performs 550 functions every second to keep us alive. We begin to think about elimination. I've had many clients that had 1 bowel movement in several days. Pain medication, in particular, can be toxic and affect bowel movements. You should have at least 2 quality bowel movements daily, light brown in color and the texture of toothpaste. If you are experiencing diarrhea or constipation, something's wrong. Lack of fiber is frequently the culprit. Many Americans get about 10 grams of fiber every day. The goal should be 25 grams. A good rule of thumb is a cup of fruit is about 2 grams of fiber, 1 cup of vegetables is about 3 grams of fiber and 1 cup of beans is 7 grams of fiber. This is only an average, but note that meat doesn't have any fiber and a lot of junk food loaded with sugar doesn't have fiber either. As you can see, Americans consume very little fiber and pay the price. Billions of dollars are spent every year on laxatives, heartburn medication and pain relievers in retail stores and billions more spent with doctors and surgeries. It is an epidemic and certainly a major problem for mental health. You also want to eat foods that are 60 or below on the Glycemic Index. Americans eat a high sugar, processed food diet which strongly contributes to most diseases.

Where do we begin? Let's start with detoxification. Most of us are toxic. I was so bad several years ago, I couldn't sleep or think straight. I was completely out of control. The following suggestions helped me: I recommend a product called "The Cleaner" I bought at the Vitamin Shoppe for about $15. You take several pills a day for 7 days. You will probably need to rest, drink a lot of water to flush out all the toxins that will be detoxed and be prepared for several trips to the bathroom. This product will help you detox every organ in your body.

The next step is to drink three (24 ounce) glasses of water every day. I recommend buying an ionic water shower head from Amazon (they have many choices for about $20). Not only will showers be much more enjoyable with this shower head, but the water is alkaline, which is important. Dr. Otto Warburg won the Nobel Prize because he proved that disease cannot thrive in an alkaline pH. Showering in alkaline water is very healthy. I also recommend pouring water from the ionic water shower into a filtered pitcher, such as Britta for instance. There are companies that are selling ionic water systems for $7000 and by buying an ionic shower head for $20, you will have accomplished ionic water at a great savings. Many people have acidic pH and this is a problem that often leads to sickness and disease. Alkaline pH also happens to be the pH most healthy foods are. Your blood is always slightly alkaline, or about 7.3 pH. You can be healthier when you bring your total body pH to a similar number.

Almost 80% of Americans are dehydrated. I know, drinking enough water for many people can be hard, even impossible. We are about 65% water and being hydrated is extremely important. You can go almost 3 months without food, but you can only last about 3 days without water. Because of poor diet, many people carry a lot of water, but are still dehydrated. Drinking water is also one of the best things you can do to curb appetite and lose weight. A good solution if you have a hard time getting the water down is to drink Celestial Seasonings Fruit Tea. It is delicious, calorie free, very nutritious and will help you get the water you need. I drink 4 cups a day on most days and you'll find teas such as chamomile and hibiscus in fruit tea are extremely healthy.

After detoxification, getting hydrated and raising your pH, the next step is the Smoothie. The smoothie will be the center of your wellness program. This smoothie is so healthy, you could literally eat nothing else all day and be satisfied. The vitamins, minerals, digestive enzymes, probiotics, protein, low glycemic carbohydrates, healthy fats and antioxidants in this smoothie are outstanding.

The Smoothie

Garden of Life Raw Organic Meal (cacao) - 1 scoop
Nutrex Hawaiian Spirulina – 1 tablespoon
Navitas Cacao (dark chocolate) – 3 tablespoons
 Almond milk – 4 ounces
Pomegranate Juice – 8 ounces
Add Fresh Bananas, Mangoes or Berries

Mix in a blender and drink every morning

Before bed, take 250 mg or 1 capsule of chelated magnesium. If sleep is difficult, try 5 mg of melatonin. Chelated magnesium is needed for over 300 biochemical reactions in your body, important for your heart and will help you relax and sleep better.

Refer to chapter 14 – Earthing – you will learn how to ground yourself and improve your health. You can improve sleep, reduce pain, improve blood flow and detoxify according to scientific research when you ground. I bought my grounding pads from Amazon for $30. Be sure to go to grounded.com to watch videos and better understand the miracle of grounding or earthing.

Americans eat too much, especially junk food. Junk food addiction is by far the biggest addiction in America today. I am a recovering junk food addict and this plan is how I beat it and how you can do it too. The best shopping plan is recommended from William Lee, MD Harvard University and I have listed it on my website, "discoverthealignmentfocusedlife.com" in an article called "40 Foods 4 Fitness." These foods are the healthiest foods you can eat. Foods such as blueberries, dark chocolate, mangoes and pomegranates are recommended and these foods are full of vitamins, minerals and antioxidants but you probably won't find them at your local restaurants. Many of these foods can go in your blender though and if you eat organic foods, such as Amy's from your local grocery store (everything from pizza, chili, Oriental food to Mexican food) you won't go hungry or broke. Buying healthy food should be your first priority and then reduce restaurant food and do intermittent fasting to save money and improve your health. Drinking ionic water is also a healthy way to save money. Besides, if you eat the right foods, drink ionic water, take healthy supplements, drink the smoothie and practice intermittent fasting, you'll not only save money on restaurant food, but you could save time and money on medicine and visits to the doctor's office.

Drinking tea is also not a bad idea. The people from Okinawa, Japan are the longest living people in the world and they are tea drinkers, especially green tea. The next popular beverage in the world after water is tea. Green tea, in particular, is proven to help with weight loss and is excellent for your immune system. I drink tea most days and highly recommend it. I also recommend drinking fruit tea (Celestial Seasonings) every day because it is very nutritious, delicious and calorie free.

Only 10% of Americans exercise, but billions of dollars are spent every year on exercise equipment and gym memberships. The problem is that we don't use the memberships or equipment. I think eBay would go out of business if people actually used their equipment instead of selling it as used on eBay.

I personally found rowing the easiest exercise and best exercise to do. I bought a machine for less than $100 on Amazon (Sunny). No more excuses. It fits nicely in my bedroom so exercise is available 24 hours a day. The first rule of management – eliminate all excuses. Rowing, swimming and walking are all great exercises. The best exercise is the one you'll do……. Every time I had a client with depression or anxiety, I would recommend exercise. Movement is critical and lack of movement is the quickest way to decompensate.

The "Blue Zones" were first reported around 2000 in National Geographic. There are 5 areas around the world that are believed to be home to the healthiest, happiest people who live the longest. These people live in Italy, Greece, Costa Rica, Loma Linda, California and Okinawa, Japan. What they have in common is that they eat primarily real food, not junk food, are very social, walk frequently and have an optimistic attitude. Life is so much easier when you're healthy. Interestingly, it's not drugs and surgery that are helping these people live past 100 years. It's healthy diet, exercise and an active social life. Americans spend a fortune on drugs and surgery and are not living longer or better. THE ALIGNMENT IS WELLNESS.

Chapter 9 – Born Again

This is not a chapter of spiritual rebirth and I'm not a "holy roller," however this chapter represents the most difficult period of my life when everything I believed and desired during my life was either accomplished or never going to happen. Even harder to swallow, I discovered I was wrong and I had to eat a huge serving of humble pie, which tastes horrible. I can tell you it's a painful feeling to think you have all the answers and your life carefully laid out only to realize you have been dreaming and one day the dream is over and you suddenly don't know who you are or what really matters anymore. My life basically sucked and I was the last one to find out. Everybody knew my life sucked and I sucked, but they did the polite thing and kept quiet or told others. If only I was a mind reader.

"I'm Brian and I'm a dreamaholic." I was self-medicating with junk food and the walls began to close in as I realized there is no AA or NA for dreamaholics. There are no 30 meetings in 30 days and there are no 30-day treatment centers for guys like me. My drug of choice was fantasy and I was always a star in my world. My marriage, my family, my career, my life savings and 3 college degrees meant absolutely nothing now. This is the story you rarely hear about. Many marriages fail in this country and the parents' relationship with their children may deteriorate. Our lives often don't look a whole lot like my parents' lives. Psychologists say we have moved from the "We generation" of my parents, the "Me generation" I have lived through and we label the kids today as the "Entitlement generation." The world is changing.

Divorce was so painful for me and I believe it is ripping our nation a part, so much so, that I wanted to write a chapter on this subject. After 26 years of marriage, the sweet girl whom I fell in love with, served me with divorce papers. The most awful day of my life. I will never forget the "little man" who came to my office and served me. I was dumbfounded, speechless and in shock. I didn't know what to say or do. For the first time in my life, I was completely without words.

The following year was filled with anger and doing everything I could do to make her angry. We call this "narcissistic rage." I didn't know it yet, but I was a narcissist. A selfish, prideful, egomaniacal asshole. Most narcissists are very well liked, except by those people who have to live with them. My wife summed it up in one sentence, "You are very inconsiderate" This was her way of saying, "You're basically a selfish asshole." I have a feeling if you are female, reading this, you are married to, have had a boyfriend or know someone with this dreaded disease. Narcissism is an epidemic and many people from the entitlement generation are living for a party of one. It was a rare problem with my parent's generation - The "we generation" had to get along to survive. It was the only way they could make it through World War II and rebuild this nation.

Why do so many marriages and families fail? What's missing? I think the first thing to ask yourself is what's really important? What are your priorities? In my opinion, relationships, health and finances are the most important things in life. When the dust settled and I honestly evaluated myself in these 3 areas, I gave myself an F in each category. It was hard to admit, but I honestly was never cognizant of my priorities and what was necessary so I could give myself an A. It became like a college course to me and I needed to know what was on the test so I could get a good grade.

Relationships begin with a concept most of us have heard about and few of us really understand. It is something called "love". I promise you, no matter how much stuff you have during your lifetime, you're not going to be able to pile it in a U-Haul and bring it to your grave site. You can't take it with you. That's certainly what I was doing. I was working too many hours and not making enough money. I was much closer than I realized to a mansion in the ground. It gets mighty lonely in that mansion and you don't have to worry about your property holding its value. It's a permanent retirement home.

LOVE IS A VERB. Love is an action word. Love is not a noun – person, place or thing. You don't have to find "the perfect man or woman," you don't need to find your soul mate and you don't have to find the one person on this planet that was made for you. YOU HAVE TO KNOW YOURSELF AND LOVE YOURSELF. How do you do that? Love is accepting who you are and appreciating your warts and bad habits. You didn't create you so stop blaming yourself for your perceived shortcomings. I believe your creator loves you and accepts you unconditionally. You don't have to prove anything to anyone. You just have to accept and love yourself as you are. I guarantee you that you aren't perfect and neither is anyone else.

When you've truly accepted and love yourself then share your love with someone else. This is the process of being born again and walking away from the world's unreachable and changing standards. Even if you do achieve those standards, they will change, people will change and you will change.

Alignment is accepting yourself, the person you want to align with and their needs so you can appropriately share your love with them. A baby, teenager, co-worker, spouse, friend, parent – there are so many different relationships and each one requires different alignment. You don't have to be in a perfect relationship as long as mutual alignment exists. The "born again" mentality insinuates that it is actually natural for you to focus on your needs and respect the person whom you were born to be……. considerate, grateful and humble. Everyone wants those qualities in their mate, but they are so rare to find. We have to surrender to the person "we want to be." If you don't love yourself, how can you love someone else? Use the concept Rick Warren discussed in "The Purpose Driven Life." Understand your SHAPE. Your Spiritual Gifts, Heart, Abilities, Personality and Experiences. Knowing yourself is called insight and loving and accepting yourself will lead to satisfactory relationships and alignment.

Admittedly, there is that "spark" that is unexplainable that brings a couple together, but why question it.

Only babies with dirty diapers like change, but we adults resist change. Perhaps the prospect of being born again and abandoning the beliefs and behaviors that just aren't working, is the best approach. You have to forgive yourself and accept yourself. Don't depend on anyone else to make you complete, love is a verb and it begins by accepting yourself, loving yourself unconditionally and then aligning your love with someone else. No one should be able to hurt you if you accept and love yourself.

Intimate relationships begin with trust, communication and respect. Trust is often the hardest thing to gain and the easiest thing to lose. Trust requires transparency and open communication called assertiveness. Assertiveness is the process of saying what you mean and meaning what you say. It is not passive or aggressive. It usually means to not wait, but say it now. The right tone of voice for assertiveness is medium, non-threatening and clear, but not passive either. Assertiveness requires the absolute truth, even when there is temporary pain. The truth will always set you free. GOOD COMMUNICATION BUILDS GOOD TRUST.

Respect comes from maintaining an acceptable lifestyle. Many of us never think about our values and morals, but when you write them down and then lead your life accordingly, you will gain self-respect and many people will also respect you. The biggest challenge will come when your morals or values are challenged and you may be forced to do what's unpopular, but in the end, most of us want to have a legacy where we can have self-respect and the satisfaction that we shunned the easy, popular way and took the journey of self-respect.

Many years later, I am still divorced. The pain of divorce, separation, loss, a stroke and 5-month coma, the bitter hardship of adjusting to a lonely life and accepting that many people will view my life as a failure still exists today. The pain drove me to severe depression and anxiety and I had to literally learn to walk, drive, eat and sleep again. I literally started over.

The amazing miracle that occurred in my darkest hour was being "born again." After I was totally sure I was dead, or wanted to be, my life began to slowly change. When I surrendered, chose love, wellness and prosperity as goals for myself and actually began to love myself and then align my new love with other people; suddenly I liked myself and other people liked me. I finally became a "real doctor" who wasn't concerned with my ego, but was genuinely concerned with their happiness. No more diagnoses, no more drugs, no more ultra-expensive treatment programs and no more meetings. I just began to share my love, listen to them and offer help. The new Brian was somebody I actually liked and trusted. Amazingly, if I trusted me, so would someone else. That is the secret to happiness. You already have everything you need. You don't have to find love; you can have it right where you are. Accept yourself, love yourself and then begin to listen. You have 2 ears and 1 mouth. LISTEN TWICE AS MUCH AS YOU TALK. Everyone just needs to be heard.

Chapter 10 – Hoping for a Miracle

Several years ago, I was hoping for a miracle. Everything I thought was right, was wrong. The path to a miracle can often be very uncomfortable. Sometimes you're afraid, even scared to death and feel all alone. Where do you turn? It is often not the path of least resistance, but the most difficult journey is walking one step at a time and not knowing where you're going, who you can trust and what does the finish line look like? Miracles rarely happen when things are comfortable and predictable. Most of us need a miracle when things are really bad and we feel lost and confused. In 2008, I needed a miracle.

Are you at a place in your life where finances, health or relationships are not working? Are you lost, lonely, afraid or frustrated? Maybe you're just stuck and have lost your way. Miracles often happen when things are uncomfortable because we realize that we simply don't have the answers and we have to trust our higher power.

When you look back at your life, I'm sure you've had mentors, role models or special friends that guided you through challenging times. I'm asking you now to let me be your mentor who's been where you are now and let me help you.

After seeing clients for 30 years, I noticed that most of them did not know what their priorities are and they always impressed me as being confused and overwhelmed. Life for them was a process of putting 10 pounds of stuff in their 5-pound bag. Many of them approached life in a circular fashion, much like the dog chasing his tail, rather than a straight line and proceeding carefully. There is an old saying, "the journey of a thousand miles begins with one step at a time." Most of us don't realize that our Creator is all we need until we get to a point in our life where he's all we have. I was there.

Sometimes, you have to lose yourself to find yourself. Believe it or not, it can be the best thing to happen to you. Many of us need to "reboot" because what we thought was right or what we wanted just wasn't working out. Rebooting is getting out of that dysfunctional program and not trying to make it work. There's nothing wrong with moving on when needed. Staying in a relationship that isn't working, a job that just doesn't feel right or diving into the cesspool you call your finances is overwhelming and is saying to you......It's time to reboot.

Fear, anger and pride are the major reasons why you stay on the merry-go-round and never get off. You don't get better; you just get older. You have to let go and refocus. You can always come back to something that needs to be addressed if you are truly hoping for a miracle because life has become so overwhelming.

Rebooting involves retracing your steps as to what's important and how you got here. You didn't create you, so quit hating the characteristics that make you.... you. Accept you and realize that when you start living your purpose based on who you are, you will feel satisfied and prosperous. You don't need someone else's approval to be you. There is only one of you. Your creator made you to be who you are and when you begin to understand that awesome person in the mirror, you will gain confidence and self-assurance.

Life is not a competition. You just have to stay in your lane and accept that you are only in the race of life for a few years and you're not going to drag all the cool awards, houses, cars and stuff you've bought over the years to your grave site. Winning or losing the race is just a ticket back to where you came from in the first place.

When you've finally hit bottom, good. What else can happen? Being stuck in the middle is the hell most of us live with every day. Crashing and burning makes you realize that you can survive and it's not the end of the world. Pain made me stronger.... much stronger. You can be the miracle by facing the fire and spitting in it. Mistakes and failures are only the path to success. I am very successful because I have made so many mistakes. Thomas Edison failed a thousand times before he finally invented the light bulb over a hundred years ago. Albert Einstein failed his college entrance exam and then went on to become the greatest physicist ever. Abraham Lincoln failed at everything he tried until in 1861, he was elected President of the United States. Failure is often the path to success.

When you focus on your priorities, you realize that life is a complicated game of Solitaire. You're playing yourself and there's no one else's approval you need. It's a one-way road to the finish line and you want to stay focused on aligning your relationships with love, honoring your body as a temple or holy place and pursue a live it, not a diet. Prosperity is a state of mind and lifestyle that requires the elimination of debt, following a budget and learning to give, not just take. Love, Wellness and Prosperity are the miracle we all want.

Conflict Resolution

Resolving conflict is the key to a successful marriage, friendship, parenting and work relations. In other words, life. Most of us have a great deal of trouble resolving conflict which is why you may come to see a doctor like me for an hour a week to state your case and verbally wrestle until someone either quits or feels like a winner. There is a better way and both parties can win. Follow the suggestions below and you can avoid the frustration and anxiety that often is produced by conflict. Remember, both parties started out on a good note and then things went terribly wrong along the way. Following the steps below will give you traction and help you get out of the mud.

1. Pray for wisdom
2. Admit my faults first
3. Listen for hurt – give good eye contact
4. Seek the truth – with love
5. Fix the problem, not the blame (blame is to b - lame)
6. Focus on reconciliation, not resolution
7. Disagree without being disagreeable
8. Winning is not the goal, peace and harmony are
9. Seek to understand before being understood
10. Make the first move when ready

One of the best things you can say if this is a lover's quarrel – "I WAS ONLY THINKING OF MYSELF"

The path to a miracle is uncomfortable. Miracles never happen in your comfort zone. My life is a miracle and I sincerely hope your life becomes a miracle also.

Chapter 11 – You Need Hope to Cope

Many of us live our lives on auto pilot. We don't think a great deal about the deck of cards we've been handed, we just play them. Often times, we want to give back some cards we were dealt only to find out we can't and we have to learn to play with the cards we really don't want. We don't like the way we look, we're not smart enough, we weren't that great in school, or family history is less than what we wanted, but it's what we inherited. We weren't born with a silver spoon, but instead we were given plastic forks. Life can be unfair and when you believe you're standing at the end of the line; you begin to lose hope. The view from the end of the line is hardly technicolor, but more like black and white.

Reality is that hardly anyone has been dealt a perfect hand. You've got to know when to hold them and when to fold them, as Kenny Rogers told us in the famous song, "The Gambler." It's not what you started with but what you finish with that really matters. YOU CAN CURSE THE DARKNESS OR LIGHT A CANDLE.

Coping skills are techniques you can use to handle difficult situations, such as depression, anxiety, stress, conflict, feeling overwhelmed, anger, confusion, grief, abandonment, abuse, financial difficulties and other problems that may drive you to see a shrink like me because you feel stuck and need help. You need hope to cope. Staying in your lane can be good advice, but what exactly is your lane? Can you define it?

The first step in dealing with trauma or just feeling like you've hit a brick wall is to stop, relax and remember where you came from. You really don't know where you came from do you? You just appeared as a zygot in your mother's womb and then were hatched about 9 months later. That's what most of us think. I'll bet you didn't come out of your mother's womb feeling depressed, anxious or overwhelmed. You just wanted breast milk and a diaper change. You were a cheap date. What happened in the years since? Why did all these problems come up and how did you get so emotionally messed up? What went wrong?

We've covered this first step before, but focus on your priorities. I only have 3 priorities in my life: quality relations, wellness and prosperity. Life can be very simple if you want it to be. Fulfilling these 3 priorities for me is the equivalent of breast milk and a diaper change at birth. It is very satisfying when I stay focused and in alignment with my priorities. When I try to do too much or lose focus, I become unhappy or worse.

Most of us tend to learn coping skills from the people we grew up with. There are very few classes taught in school for coping skills. It's only when stuff hits the fan, problems arise or the need to change comes about, we look for coping skills. They can be the answer to what may seem to be unsolvable problems at the time.

Here's a list of coping mechanisms that will help you when you are feeling overwhelmed and they can help you be more resilient and stress tolerant.

1. Writing, painting, drawing or photography
2. Play an instrument, singing or dancing
3. Take a hot shower or bath
4. Take a walk or go for a drive
5. Gardening or Farming
6. Watch a movie
7. Play a game
8. Go shopping
9. Organize your home
10. Read
11. Take a vacation

12. Talk to someone you trust
13. Set good boundaries and say no when you need to
14. Write a letter to someone you care about
15. Be assertive (say what you mean and mean what you say)
16. Spend time with people you care about
17. Serve someone in need (volunteer)
18. Encourage others
19. Make a list of everything you are grateful for
20. Focus on your priorities
21. Forgive yourself
22. Reward yourself
23. Set realistic expectations
24. Be flexible
25. Write a list of your strengths
26. Get enough sleep and eat healthy (avoid junk food)
27. Exercise
28. Enjoy nature
29. Prioritize tasks
30. Cut back on your schedule, eliminate unnecessary tasks

Coping mechanisms can contribute to coping skills when you practice them. Most of the time, when we are depressed, anxious or feeling overwhelmed, we want to retreat. Retreating to the bedroom, refrigerator or TV is a recipe for disaster. I know…. you just don't feel like doing anything. Sometimes the first step is to resolve the physical requirements to reduce stress or improve mood. I love the Smoothie (recipe in this book) to pick up my spirits. Your body needs 14 vitamins, 68 minerals, 3 fats, 25 grams of daily fiber and digestive enzymes to function properly. Sometimes you may be toxic and need a colonic irrigation treatment or a good massage. Sometimes you need rest or peaceful sleep. Grounding is a wonderful way to relax, sleep better and relieve pain. Exercise is also an excellent way to look and feel better. If you're not right physically, it's hard to concentrate or even cope.

Many people need to learn to set limits. Most of us take on too much and we become the jack of all trades but master of none. Learn to say NO. It's tempting to say yes. There are so many possibilities, but most of the time, it's a matter of not knowing exactly what you want, unable to resist temptation and then getting over your head. Especially, when it comes to debt. The average American is $20,000 in debt plus a mortgage if he owns a home. Debt is the #1 reason for divorce in America.

The journey of a thousand miles begins with one step at a time. Alignment requires focus. Get one thing right then move on to the next thing. Don't juggle several balls at a time just to prove you can. That may work for a minute, but eventually you're going to drop all of those balls and then it's like putting the toothpaste back into the tube, once it's been squeezed out.

Coping is hoping. We all want hope in our life, but when we feel overwhelmed, life becomes hopeless. Remember that baby you started out as not wanting anything but breast milk and a diaper change. Often times, you are manipulated by the media, internet and a society that breeds stress. I've travelled around the world and America is one of the most stressful countries I've ever been in. Our diet is terrible, we don't handle money well, we're all living our lives with the focus on NEXT and MORE. Marriages, relationships, jobs, everything is either dismissed or traded in for what's NEXT or adding MORE will solve all of our problems. Unfortunately, the bill will always come due and has to be paid. There are only so many things that can just be "charged." Stress and conflict are not free and can be very costly.

The best alignment for coping with your life is to avoid NEXT and MORE and focus on quality relationships that begin with accepting and loving yourself and then aligning your love with another person. You get off the relationship merry-go-round and stop searching for the perfect mate who is right around the corner.

Love yourself first and you will find that everyone is attracted to love. Then, focus on helping others. How many people do you know are givers and not takers? You're still trying to think of somebody, but maybe you weren't attracted to people you remember as givers, such as parents, siblings, pastors or others, but you were attracted to their humility and kindness. Givers are the tortoises and takers are the hares in the race of life. The givers take longer and may experience more push back, but in the long run, they win. The best part is that givers like themselves and it feels good to give. It's how we're built.

Negative coping skills can be very harmful and they are really only strategies to avert or avoid stressful situations and they usually make things worse. The following is a list of negative behaviors:

1. Procrastination
2. Drug or Alcohol Abuse
3. Wasting time
4. Blaming others
5. Isolating or withdrawing
6. Mean or distasteful jokes
7. Gossip
8. Criticizing
9. Lying
10. Sabotaging
11. Provoking violence
12. Denial
13. Inflexibility
14. Suicide
15. Gambling
16. Eating Junk food

Often times, it may seem that when you engage in negative coping mechanisms you literally feel you are going backwards. It doesn't feel like forward movement or progress, because it isn't.

The alignment is avoidance, escape or simple poor attempts that have no chance of solving the problem. You aren't coping, you're lost, confused or frustrated.

The following steps will get you on track to solve the problem.

1. Accept the fact you have stuffed 10 pounds of stuff in a 5-pound bag (be selective)
2. Know your priorities and what's REALLY important
3. Realize it will take several steps to get to the finish line
4. Relax knowing that everyone's been where you are – and many succeed!
5. Copy whatever has already worked
6. Be realistic – it's OK to say NO or start over
7. Keep your eyes on the prize (ignore the other stuff)
8. Live one day at a time
9. Be thankful for every bit of progress (no matter how small)
10. See the problem already solved

You need hope to cope but take the time to find resolution. Too many times, things that need to be said are not said and things that need to be done are left undone. Have the courage to do the right thing and be assertive. Unfinished business should not be put off or delayed. Do it now and achieve resolution. Coping skills will help you achieve results!

Chapter 12 -Addiction: Life from the Neck Up

"Insanity is doing the same thing over and over again and expecting DIFFERENT results. Albert Einstein"

Most of us are narrowly focused from the neck up. If it tastes good, smells good, looks good and feels good....... we're interested. Every addiction is focused from the neck up. We need taste, smell, sight or feelings to fully appreciate any addiction. Junk food addiction, alcoholism, cigarette smoking and drug addiction live above the neck and I would prove that point to every client that came through my program. I would sit my clients in a circle and ask them to put a black bag over their heads. I would then ask them…Can anyone smell, taste, see or feel anything right now? They always answered no and said they felt lost because everything that mattered in their life was inaccessible. I would then ask, "Can anyone smoke a cigarette, drink a beer, do some drugs or eat some junk food? The answer was of course, no. They were paralyzed. I would then say, can you be an addict right now? They quickly realized they were totally helpless and even felt useless. They were watching their lives pass before their eyes and felt completely worthless.

I said, now that I've got your attention, is it absolutely clear that all addictions occur and are maintained from the neck up? Without your head, your addiction is over. I told them that I wanted them to focus from the neck down. I pointed out that the liver, on their right side just below the shoulder, was working to provide 550 functions to keep them alive. I asked, "What do you provide your liver" The answer from them was obvious. They would say," We feed our liver junk food, cigarette smoke, alcohol and drugs. We're destroying our liver." I went on to remind them that the heart, bowels, kidneys and intestines are below the liver taking care of them right now and they are polluting and abusing their organs. All the activities that are important and matter are taking place below the neck and they have taken them for granted.

I made my clients wear the black bags for 30 minutes to feel the pain, emptiness and discomfort that helped them realize that addiction is from the neck up and when they gave their body attention from the neck down, things began to change. Only babies with dirty diapers like change, but these addicts were starting to see that all of the AA meetings and psychiatric medicines were virtually useless until they realized that the problem was from the neck up and total unappreciation for what the rest of the body does is what fuels denial and perpetuates relapse. Less than 10% of addicts in treatment, often paying $60,000 per month, recover successfully. Over 90% relapse and I had clients that told me they had been in over 30 different treatment centers.

> *"About 80% of my clients had experienced trauma in their lifetime, often as a child. A history of abuse, trauma, abandonment, grief, separation or pain from living in a divorced family is typical in most drug and alcohol treatment centers. The majority of clients had deep, dark secrets and had been self-medicating for years. I had clients with problems that spanned 40 years. Trauma doesn't just go away on its own and many clients don't want to do the work to stop self-medicating and recover."*
> *- Trauma Therapy (Sylvia's Secret)*

Trauma is a complex and painful side of addictions therapy that many centers never adequately address. As I mentioned earlier, the majority of addiction clients have suffered deep personal issues, often from their childhood, that stimulated them to self-medicate and prompted an endless trail of failures, addiction, unsatisfactory relationships, hiding from the painful feelings of abuse, abandonment, unresolved grief, a dysfunctional family and childhood and ultimately denial and the perpetual effort to make relationships, jobs or even life work. Pills, therapists, treatment centers or recovery groups become a futile effort to mask the pain of trauma and unfortunately the client never quite makes it to the finish line explaining the misery they endured, often for years, just to be disappointed…. never reaching resolution or recovery.

Typically, there are two common therapy models used for trauma: EMDR, which utilizes a light and bar the client holds to keep the client engaged and able to withstand the painful process of facing the trauma they experienced, often years ago.

The other form of trauma therapy, the one I did with all of my clients, is called psychodrama. It was one of the most dynamic and effective therapy models I have ever used. I will explain an actual client I had, what she went through and how psychodrama worked for her. In my 30 years of clinical experience, I can honestly say that other individual, group or family therapy models would have never achieved the results I saw with Sylvia. It was absolutely incredible.

Sylvia was a 58-year-old female from New Jersey who had been an alcoholic for most of her adult life. She was married for 34 years and had two kids now in their early 30's. Sylvia had a secret and hadn't told anyone…...ever. It was time for our psychodrama group and about 8 clients would attend each group. They stayed with each other in this treatment program which was called a PHP or Partial Hospitalization Program. Sylvia stayed with the clients for the entirety of the 30-day program. The clients became familiar with each other and often felt comfortable opening up and sharing their deepest secrets. Sylvia had a secret she had kept for 40 years. No one…...no one, including her husband of 34 years, her 2 kids and even her mother was completely aware of exactly what Sylvia had experienced and caused her to self-medicate and drown herself in alcohol due to the shame and pain she had experienced her entire adult life. Everything was a charade, an act, trying to be a good mother, wife and employee, but struggling every single day to find even a shred of self-esteem.

Sylvia was too proud and too afraid to commit suicide, but she wanted to, many times. She worried about her husband, her kids and what everyone would think and then she would drown her worries, fears and doubts in a bottle and apologize always bearing the burden of guilt and worry, hoping that someone would understand her, truly love her and forgive her. Many people who have been abused as children blame themselves. She had nothing to do with it, but it was still her fault.

Sylvia was sexually abused, raped, by her father every day of her life from age 12 to age 18 until she could leave this nightmare called home. This was her father.... how could he be guilty? How could her father do this to her, she must have done something wrong? She wanted to earn her father's love, but she also hated him and hated every day she had to come home. Sylvia was raped, trapped and forced to endure daily sex with her father who carefully blamed her, never taking responsibility for his actions and never showing any concern for his daughter's feelings. It would ruin the rest of her life until, at age 58, she came to my office and finally made herself available to face this nightmare that had haunted her for 40 years.

I've had many clients over the years who had been sexually abused, but nothing quite this graphic and disturbing. My heart hurt for Sylvia and I wondered how anyone could rape his own daughter for her entire teenage years and make her think it was her fault. Never did I sit in my office and look across my desk at a woman who had been abused daily for 6 years, 40 years ago. I prayed that night telling God that I felt overwhelmed, angry as hell at her father and I could only cry every time I thought about Sylvia. I was paralyzed and felt unable to know exactly how I could help her.

The next day in the psychodrama group, eight clients sat around the circle and Sylvia sat at the end and I was directly behind her. There were 3 chairs and Sylvia sat in the first chair on the right. This was her childhood (ages 2 -12) and I asked her to share all of her memories from that age in school, home, church, friends, anything she could remember. The first chair was rather quiet and uneventful. The group didn't have any comments so we had a quick break and then she moved over to the 2nd chair (ages 13 – 19). These were the adolescent years and I asked her to share memories from school, relatives, church, jobs and home. After a few minutes, Sylvia began to cry and scream. She remembered every horrible minute and was literally transformed to her teenage years. She was ready, after 40 years, to tell everything. She was so sick of carrying the horrible guilt and finally felt comfortable sharing everything. She couldn't take it anymore. The fear, the hate and the anger all surfaced and Sylvia screamed so hard her lungs hurt and she cried until there no were no more tears. She faced her worst nightmare. She felt terrified.

It took 2 days and 3 therapists to help Sylvia recount every nightmare that had been haunting her for 40 years and had caused her to lose countless hours of sleep, endure many drunken nights and live through so many AA meetings that never helped. Now she had to tell her husband a 40-year-old secret.

Family therapy was a process that involved calling her husband back in New Jersey, airing out feelings and gauging his support. Before the session, I asked Sylvia if she was ready to tell her husband what she had revealed in group, because after 34 years he still didn't know his father-in-law had raped his wife every day as a teenager and their two children did not know Sylvia's secret either.

Sylvia agreed to tell him. She was ready to face the consequences because she was so tired of living a lie and keeping an ugly secret for so many years. She really believed the truth would set her free. She was ready.

I had never met her husband so we were literally starting from scratch. What a way to start a therapy session, but Sylvia was ready. I started the session and then I asked Sylvia if she wanted to share anything with her husband. She courageously told him everything and as you could imagine, he was furious. He screamed and said, "I'm going to kill that son of a bitch." Sylvia's father lived nearby and was 81 years old. I told her husband that as horrible as this was, it happened 40 years ago. He had to move on with Sylvia and he could at least understand why she was self-medicating. I told them one of the hardest things to do was to forgive, but when you do you will have closure. Sylvia's father didn't deserve forgiveness, none of us really do, but we all deserve to be set free from a 40-year nightmare, such as the one Sylvia was experiencing.

I knew it was difficult for Sylvia to accept that she had been violated by her father all those years ago and she felt unclean, especially with her husband. I told Sylvia that every cell in her body renews in 7 years. That is a scientific fact. In other words, the Sylvia who was raped as a teenager no longer exists. Her body has totally renewed and essentially cleansed itself of the horrible nightmare she endured 40 years ago.

Sylvia finally forgave herself and even forgave her father. She let go and moved on with her life. She had faced her greatest fear and for the first time in her adult life, she felt free and loved. Her husband, mother and children, after many difficult days, finally was able to forgive and come to Sylvia's aid. For the first time in her life, she had faced the demons.

Chapter 13 – Shoulding and Musturbating

The tyranny of the "shoulds" and "musts" was first predicted almost 80 years ago by Dr. Karen Horney who was an early cognitive therapist, meaning that she was focused on how we think, rather than how we act. She said the "tyranny of the shoulds" handicapped us with cognitive dissonance or what we call "stinking thinking" today and causes us to miss out on opportunities and leads to many emotional problems.

"Stinking thinking" often first appears in youth when we are compared to siblings, classmates or friends. We believe we "should" be stronger, better looking, smarter, faster or simply better than we are or we are just less than everyone else. The problem with the rat race is first revealed during these early years in our life…... the rats are winning. Cognitive dissonance or stinking thinking becomes the seeds of depression, anxiety and low self-esteem. We never seem to live up to our parents, teachers or other authority figure's expectations and we ultimately resign to feelings of failure which becomes depression.

The shoulds are often a large part of our life and the really sad reality is that we don't even know how they became such major influences in our life. No one does. Everyone, parents, teachers, friends, may start out innocent enough and honestly believe that certain expectations and behaviors are actually helpful or the "right" thing to do, but when we reject them, don't understand them or simply want something else, they may force negative thoughts with the illogical belief that we "should" act, think or behave a certain way to be accepted. It is particularly difficult with people who have control problems or strong needs for control. Unfortunately, the shoulds may trigger poor grades, avoidance, disappointment or social unrest. It's particularly difficult for children who don't know how to express themselves or are afraid to express themselves. Often times, they simply aren't ready for assertive expression yet.

Problems caused by the shoulds during childhood manifest as much deeper and more pervasive issues as adults. Sexual confusion, acting out behavior, rebellion, drug abuse, or criminal behavior can all result as unresolved issues and feelings evolving from the need to "fit in", believing you are not getting approval of important figures in your life or believing you are a failure. Self -esteem can plummet and is often very fragile during childhood. More suicide attempts occur during adolescence. I have witnessed and been involved as a therapist with many adolescents who were suicidal. Drugs and alcohol will usually magnify the situation and when parents are uninvolved, poor role models or are confused, it can be lethal.

The shoulds" often intensify with age and become "musts" and the musts are stronger and harder to work with when doing therapy. Many clients feel hopeless and helpless and very unstable. The average college student will change his or her major 7 times. Many young people have a hard time completing and finishing tasks. The NEXT and MORE approach to life often begins in adolescence and it is just easier to say NEXT or MORE to replace a bad relationship, job or living situation. When money or opportunity is available MORE becomes the goal. More junk food, alcohol, drugs or just move on to the next thing. This is the foundation of an unstable and unpredictable life. Peace is virtually non-existent.

Cognitive therapy is about thinking or how thoughts impact your life. After Dr. Horney espoused the "Tyranny of the Shoulds", Dr. Albert Ellis gave us RET – Rational Emotive Therapy. He believed we were often irrational and warned that words and thoughts such as always or never set us up for failure. He believed it was important to be accurate and make rational statements such as, "You don't clean up your room 6 out of 7 days per week and it really bothers me. Could you try to clean it up more often?' If progress is made, it is better to reinforce the positive rather than argue about the negative. Most of us focus on the negative and it affects our relationships with our children and significant others. We need to catch kids and others doing something right and reinforce that behavior instead of focusing on what went wrong.

Dr. Fritz Perls, the father of gestalt therapy, said "I really don't trust most patients. They are basically full of elephant shit." Perls was a fanatic for honesty and truth. I did my first clinical supervision with a doctor who was a gestalt therapist. The session felt like being interrogated by a police officer under very bright lights. I could see how it could be effective at getting to the real issues, but I could also see how most patients would bolt after the first session. Perls and gestalt therapy was a bridge between Horney in the 40's and Ellis in the 80's, but therapy was becoming more popular and particularly drug and alcohol therapy was becoming very popular. AA was important when it started in the 30's, but by the time RET became popular, AA was becoming less significant. Insurance companies started paying for therapy, by the 2000's and it became the 2nd most expensive medical intervention after cancer.

As we speak, there are many tools in the tool bag for psychologists today. In my 30 years of experience in the field, I went from interpreting intelligence and personality tests to utilizing 12-step therapy with addicts, doing trauma therapy in an in-patient addiction program to doing intense psychosocial interviews which ultimately resulted in psychiatric treatment. Diagnosis for us or use of the Diagnostic and Statistics Manual (DSM -V) has evolved over the years from a multiaxial approach which encouraged therapy and addressed all areas relevant to the client's needs to an approach today tailor made for psychiatrists and medical intervention. Psychological counseling and testing have become too expensive and have very poor long term or permanent results. It has become a nightmare for medical insurance and about all that can be achieved today is a band-aid approach to patch up the patient and send them back into the cruel world as soon as possible. Most very expensive treatment centers today only have about a 5% long term success rate. Any success is usually very temporary.

Alignment is the key and most of us are either unaligned or we are aligned with something or someone that will never have lasting positive benefits. We have to forgive and let go of any baggage from our past. We all have a past. Just let go and move on. You can't fix the past and you can never completely heal the wounds. You can align yourself with the present, which is a gift. When you've turned around from watching the same painful film of the past and start living for today, you become open to the great possibilities that exist, if you just let them.

Alignment with the "shoulds and musts, typically born in your early years and matured in later years in school, jobs or relationships, can be causing depression, anxiety, drug addiction or dysfunctional behavior today and often times a desire to escape from demand causes even more problems to occur and worse, you may feel so overwhelmed, lost and confused, you can become "the deer caught in the headlights", meaning you feel completely hopeless and helpless.

Forgiveness is the best strategy to let go of the past, let go of the shoulds and musts that may have set you up for failure and begin to move forward. It's not a matter of who deserves forgiveness, we all need forgiveness, just forgive and let go. Be bigger than those people who have hurt you and focus on these words.... REMEMBER THE BEST AND FORGET THE REST.

Chapter 14 – Earthing: Alignment with Nature (Grounding)

I'm guessing you've never heard of earthing or grounding. Most people haven't. It's not a matter of if earthing will receive a Nobel Prize, it's a matter of when. It's that important and it is just now beginning to receive the notoriety it deserves. The simple explanation of grounding or earthing is that we used to be connected to the earth many years ago, but in the last 50 years or so, our lifestyle has disconnected us from the earth and it's amazing healing properties. The bottom line is that when we are grounded properly, we absorb the electrons from the earth and we become properly aligned. Our bodies have strong electrical properties and accurate voltage is often a problem with most people and it leads to poor health and disease.

Just look at an AC outlet in your house and you will notice that it consists of 3-prongs. What is the 3rd prong for? It is used for grounding. Grounding is critical with electricity and if an electrical appliance is not grounded, it can cause serious damage. Years ago, many homes had lightning rods to absorb any lightning strikes and redirect the lightning to the ground. The earth captures the lightning and uses the electrons. The earth is fully charged with electrons and can be used by us to create balance and help improve our immune system.

There are trillions of free radicals floating around your body right now. They are cells without an electron and that makes them dangerous. Free radicals can contribute to disease and aging. They impair our immune systems. When free radicals are given an electron, it neutralizes them, or makes them harmless. This is why anti-oxidants are so important. This is also why you've heard so much about oxidative stress. It is a huge problem today and contributing to sickness and premature death.

Earthing or grounding fights free radicals because when you are grounded, you are receiving the earth's natural supply of electrons that your body loves. It is the best anti-oxidant on earth. Grounding was part of life for ancient man who lived, slept on and had a close relationship with the earth. We were meant to be one with the planet and modern man has drifted so far away from nature, it has caused severe harm and rampant disease and suffering. We were not created to be put under a microscope or to simply take a "pill for our ill." We were designed to live with the earth. Our bodies are electrical machines and when voltage and current are off, we become sick or dysfunctional. It's impossible to be fully functional and completely well when we are not properly grounded. It is estimated that free radical damage can cause 22 different diseases.

The history of earthing and current knowledge starts in the 1960's when the founder of earthing was working in the cable television industry and wondered why grounding was so important for electronics but was not considered important for human health. Eventually, he found a doctor in San Diego to help him analyze the results of several people that he helped stay grounded during sleep and test the impact grounding had on their health. The results were astounding and the grounding movement began. Our founder's next step was to speak with Stephen Sinatra, MD who was a cardiologist and at the time was one of the first doctors in America to understand the relationship between inflammation and health. We know today that virtually every disease is affected by inflammation. Dr. Sinatra noted that inflammation was particularly relevant in cardiovascular disease, the nation's #1 killer.

Grounding or earthing eliminates inflammation. Dr. Sinatra helped co-author a book on earthing to explain how it neutralizes free radicals and stops inflammation. There is also a movie produced about earthing on his web site – grounded.com. The film explains in detail the process of earthing and how it can benefit you. There are also products on the web site, such as bed sheets and shoes that will help you stay grounded. There's obviously very little money in grounding, no drugs or expensive surgeries, which is why you've probably never heard of it.

We know today that inflammation is the root cause of almost every disease. When you are not grounded, similar to an electrical appliance that is not grounded, inflammation or the potential for serious problems can occur. The most common cause of death and disease in the United States is chronic disease and it is believed that inflammation is the root cause of these diseases. Grounding appears to be a natural, inexpensive, safe and easy treatment to reduce or even eliminate inflammation. Simply put, because you are not grounded, you are inflamed, which is the process of cells missing an electron. Grounding is the simple, natural process of accessing electrons from the earth through the grounding plugs in your home. The earth is full of electrons, usually obtained from lightning. Grounding has been proven with excellent results for pain, immune, sleep problems and cardiovascular issues.

Wellness is a holistic proposition, whereas medical care focuses on drugs and surgery as being the main therapy. When you ground and access the unlimited electrons in the earth, you will neutralize or effectively render free radicals harmless. You often won't be healed right away but you will neutralize free radicals when you start grounding. When the body is properly grounded and you are eating the right nutrition, your body begins to heal. I have seen chronically ill people improve dramatically, within weeks, once they begin grounding and these people were also drinking the smoothie daily listed in this book. Health often reflects alignment with the earth and our bodies are self-healing organisms when they are properly grounded, getting the right nutrition and properly detoxified.

This book is about proper alignment to simplify and enhance your life. Alignment with the earth is the original intent of our Creator and we are electrical beings who are out of alignment. Earthing or grounding can bring you back into proper alignment with Mother Earth.

Chapter 15 – The Wellness Doctor's Farmacy

Growing up, the pharmacy was a place where my family spent a lot of time and money. It was a panacea of remedies for the colds and diseases of life. Prevention was never mentioned or thought about and healthcare was left to the MD, the guy with the Magic Degree. Wellness was a term not even thought of and organic meant planting healthy crops, but not something I ever ate. We went to the grocery store and bought food prepared from (unbeknownst to us) Monsanto farms loaded with nasty chemicals and food I would never feed to my dog today. Hey, these were brands on television and in the grocery store, so they must be good. Little did we know.

Pharmacies are slowly being replaced by Farmacies today as we are more and more aware that healthy organic food is simply better and is replacing the junk food, we all grew up with. I'm sure you know that childhood diabetes and obesity are an epidemic today and completely out of control. We sure know how to make money in America, but we can spend it too and we also know how to eat junk food. The average American eats 6-10 times a day. Snacking, fast food and eating on the fly has replaced the family that stays home and prepares fresh meals.

Organic food and health food stores are slowly replacing the big chain grocery stores filled with junk food and neighborhood pharmacies. Frankly, America is catching up to the rest of the world. Many countries would never sell the stuff we call food because it's so unhealthy. Most health issues can either be prevented or treated naturally, if we know what to do. I was on several medications and told I could never get off of them because I had a serious stroke and was in a 5-month coma. I wish the doctors that told me that could see me today, but I do want to thank the doctors and nurses who helped save my life. Medicine should be more like fire stations, we're all happy to use our taxes to pay for their services, but I have never needed a fire truck in my life. Fire prevention should be the focus, but I'm still thankful for the fire fighters that are on standby every night just in case we need them. They are truly heroes to me. Health care should focus on prevention, when possible, also. Functional medicine is my choice today because these doctors are well versed in both allopathic (drugs and surgery) and homeopathic (prevention and wellness) health care. Mark Hyman, MD is a leader in functional medicine and he has many educational videos on You Tube. I believe functional medicine and wellness health care are slowly changing medicine in this country. Dr. Hyman helped start the functional medicine program at Cleveland Clinic and the Mayo Clinic has practiced functional medicine for many years. I am not advocating replacing or eliminating drugs and surgery, just focusing on prevention (as the fire department does) where saving lives and public welfare are the priorities. Unfortunately, medicine has focused on insurance and money for so long that it is time to recognize functional medicine where both allopathic and homeopathic health care will have a seat at the table.

Not only did I lose 200 pounds, but I replaced the 4 different blood pressure medications and the 6 other medications that were supposed to help my heart with natural solutions recommended by a functional medical doctor. I feel better today, I look better and I really believe I'm getting younger (healthier) every day. If your doctor feels medicines are necessary, then do what you feel is best, but you may consider seeing a functional medical doctor first and you will find they may be open to natural solutions.

The Wellness Doctor's Farmacy lists some practical, time tested natural remedies that can help you. These remedies have a long history in many cultures around the world. They are typically inexpensive and non-invasive with no side effects.

1. Digestive and gastrointestinal distress – charcoal
2. Weight Loss, slow metabolism – green tea
3. Poor energy – spirulina
4. Sleep – magnesium (chelated), melatonin. grounding
5. Inflammation – curcumin, grounding, fulvic acid
6. Depression – cacao (dark chocolate) – 3 tbsp
7. Pain – grounding, medical marijuana
8. High Blood Pressure – grape seed extract (200 mg), Dr. Sinatra (Omega Q Plus)
9. Anxiety – valerian root, grounding
10. High Blood Sugar – cinnamon, fasting (lower A1C below 7.0)

It's always best to see a functional medical doctor to ensure safety, especially if you're taking medications, but the above-mentioned herbs and natural ingredients have helped many people and are worth considering. The goal is to obtain an A1C Hemoglobin (blood sugar) score of 7.0 or below, blood pressure score of 120/80 or below and body fat percentage in the teens (more important than scale weight). Blood sugar, blood pressure and body fat percentage are three of the most important scores. Good scores from these items, proper intermittent fasting and grounding will combine to help provide good health.

I always recommend the following plan to maintain your health.

1. Detox – Fulvic Acid, The Cleaner, Fasting
2. Water – Ionic (alkaline) - at least 68 ounces per day
3. Smoothie – refer to chapter 8
4. Vegetables, Fruits – Kale, Spinach, Blueberries, Mangoes, Pomegranates, Avocadoes
5. Meal Plan – Forty Foods for Fitness (discoverthealignmentfocusedlife.com), next chapter
6. Grounding – Buy bed sheets and products from grounded.com, also on Amazon

7. Fasting – Drink smoothie (above) and then fast with water for 24 hours – lose about 1 lb. daily
8. Exercise – Rowing (30 minutes daily), walking, swimming
9. Supplements – Dr. Sinatra (Omega Q Plus), chelated magnesium, smoothie
10. Body Care – Mill Creek Organic Shampoo and Conditioner, Dr. Bonner toothpaste

Chapter 16 – 40 Foods 4 Fitness

Wellness and physical alignment require a fundamental shift in the way you think about health, particularly the food you eat. Most of us will take a pill or drink a smoothie we like, but we have trouble saying no to the foods we really want to eat, even though we know they are bad for us. When you factor in advertising, public preference, enticing smells that most restaurants and fast-food joints know make it difficult for us to turn down, junk food wins and wellness loses. The only problem with that scenario is that the losses aren't seen quickly often times and the heart attacks, strokes, diabetes, cancer and other severe medical problems may not surface for a few years, but they come and when they do it can mean horrible expense, time missed from work, pain and even death. Our generation is the first generation in America that has experienced rapid decline in health at a young age. We can get very sick, very quickly. Childhood obesity and childhood diabetes are an epidemic today and getting worse. Drinking one 6-ounce bottle of Coca-Cola was average when I was a kid. Today, the 99-ounce Big Gulp has replaced that tiny six-ounce bottle and wreaked havoc. Addition is so much easier than subtraction and taking away what we like can be a major problem. Sugar consumption has increased 800 % since the 70's and we eat twice as much as we did from that decade. SUGAR IS THE ENEMY and it is at least part of the cause of all of the major illnesses today: cancer, diabetes, heart disease, obesity and Alzheimer's.

Meal planning is often anything but planning. Meals are typically ordered on the fly, microwaved or eaten in a drive-thru. Families rarely sit down together for a meal. When I was a kid, you always sat down with your family and ate a meal together at least once every day. Now, McDonald's and fast-food restaurants have replaced parents as chefs and prepare our daily meals. There's no meal planning, there is only meal ordering from the menu. We really don't know what's in our food, but we hope it's healthy.

My colleague and I once did a study on families that ate one meal a day with their children and we discovered an 80% improvement in school attendance, behavior and grades. Kids really like to eat at home with their parents and want to be with their families. The best part of eating together once a day was their meals were planned and everyone ate so much healthier.

A good place to start is to look at people who have done a good job with meal planning, aging, wellness and overall health. A doctor in Italy identified 5 areas in the world where people live the longest and are the healthiest. He circled those areas with a blue marker and called them "The Blue Zones." This was in 2000 and a writer for the National Geographic magazine did on story on the "Blue Zones." The 5 areas were Italy, Greece, Costa Rica, Loma Linda, California and Okinawa, Japan. What did these 5 areas have in common? They ate primarily real food, not junk food, they exercised, even walked daily, they drank only moderate amounts of alcohol, had a great social life and they avoided sugar for the most part. Okinawa is where the longest living people live and the main difference was, they drank about 4 cups of green tea daily.

It was not genetics, surgeries, medicines or any medical device that Americans spend billions of dollars on every year that lengthened or improved the Blue Zones inhabitant's lives. It was real food, the absence of junk food, particularly sugar and light regular exercise that keeps them living to be 100 + years of age. More importantly, they are happier and believe their lives are more fulfilling. Amazingly, they are usually not "grounded" as you can be, not fasting which has shown enough medical promise to earn a Nobel Prize in 2016 and most are not drinking the smoothies and other things recommended in this book. The bottom line: If we learn from the Blue Zone inhabitants and utilize that knowledge and combine it with what we know today, such as fasting and grounding, we can live long and healthy lives, not to mention medical advancements may also may help. Wellness is not a placebo but a legitimate anti-aging lifestyle.

A good idea, before we get started on meal planning, is to find out what foods you are sensitive to. I recommend getting a saliva test for food sensitivities so you can be aware of what foods you need to avoid or at least be cautious about. You can go to everlywellcom and do a saliva test for $160 that will measure 96 different foods to identify the foods you are sensitive to. Eating foods, you are sensitive to, may lead to many health problems including obesity.

Below is a list of foods (organic when possible) that you were BORNED to eat and many blue zone residents are eating to help them live past 100. More importantly, your body LOVES these foods. Digestion and elimination problems will often go away!!

1. Wild Salmon
2. Pomegranates
3. Carrots
4. Kiwifruit
5. Blueberries
6. Strawberries
7. Broccoli
8. Kale
9. Spinach
10. Watermelon
11. Snacks - Organic Popcorn (Lesser Evil), Chips (Siete)
12. Peppers, Onions
13. Sweeteners (Stevia, Monk Fruit)
14. Garlic
15. Bamboo Shoots

16. Dark Chocolate (cacao)
17. Extra Virgin Olive Oil, Coconut Oil, Avocado Oil
18. Sea Salt (Himalayan)
19. Organic Coffee (2 cups maximum daily)
20. Cherries
21. Mangoes
22. Walnuts
23. Almonds
24. Green Beans
25. Green Tea, Black Tea, Chamomile Tea, Fruit Tea Sampler (Celestial Seasonings)
26. Mushrooms
27. Flax Seeds, Chia Seeds, sunflower Seeds
28. Cauliflower (pizza crust)
29. Tomatoes
30. Grapefruit
31. Avocadoes
32. Legumes – Beans, Lentils, Peas
33. Organic Free-Range Eggs
34. Sweet Potatoes (bake or boil)
35. Peaches
36. Steel Cut Oatmeal
37. Lemons, Limes
38. Sugar Free Ice Cream (Rebel) and Sugar Free Greek Yogurt (Oikos)
39. Brown Rice
40. Sourdough Bread

The all-stars are blueberries, kale, eggs, wild salmon, pomegranates, beans, avocadoes and cacao. Coconut Water, Almond milk, Fruit Tea Sampler (Celestial Seasonings) and Ionic Water are the best beverages.

This list was inspired from "Eat to Beat Disease" by William Lee, MD, Harvard University

Focusing on the above 40 foods, along with the daily smoothie with pomegranate juice and almond milk will give you the nutrition you need. The body needs earthing or grounding to utilize electrons from the earth to neutralize the free radicals in your body and frequent fasting is a great way to normalize body fat, blood pressure, blood sugar and prompts the body to produce BDNF (brain food) which will help prevent Alzheimer's and neurodegenerative diseases.

Nutrition is a science and if you apply the rules of healthy eating, you can experience the miracle of wellness.

Chapter 17 – Tough Love

From birth we learn to be self-centered and focused on self-gratification. Babies with dirty diapers like change, but babies are narrowly focused on pleasure and satisfaction. They aren't too concerned with the rest of the world, only their small space matters. As children grow older, "mine" becomes the mantra and basic lifestyle, and when mine is replaced with ours, problems occur. When children enter school, the dysfunctional behavior "negative attention seeking" begins. The child will often do anything to be recognized by friends, classmates or peers and sometimes doesn't really care how it affects others. The classic example is the student who is acting out in school just to get the attention of his classmates. He is seeking their attention, but in the teacher's view it is very negative and disruptive. The solution for the teacher is to send the student to the principal and take a time out. Kids hate time out, but it removes them from the negative attention seeking and makes them realize there are unpleasant consequences for disruptive behavior. The child can only come back to the classroom when he or she is quiet and attentive. The teacher demands compliance or else she will lose the other 30 kids in the classroom and she will lose credibility. Some might call this "tough love".

I spent over 10 years with children and their parents focused on negative behavior, parenting skills, learning assertive communication and developing positive reinforcement. Most parents are giving their children negative reinforcement because they are stressed out, overwhelmed and afraid. Being a parent isn't easy, especially when the child is your first or you are raising several children. Most of us love kids and you may want to have several kids, but things have changed and it is simply more difficult today to be an effective parent, so the discussion in this chapter is very IMPORTANT and will help make your life easier and better. The following rules will help any parent and I can tell you from raising my own children and being the therapist for many children in 30 years, these approaches work.

1. Relax, quit worrying and TRUST yourself. You've got this.
2. ALWAYS use positive reinforcement. Catch your kids doing something right and then reinforce it with kind words or something the child will appreciate. Do this often and look for positive actions you can reinforce. Do not give negative behavior attention or at least minimize it. You want your child to know that positive behavior is the answer.
3. ALWAYS use boundaries for everything. The more consistent you are the better. I worked with a foster care mother who was 78 years old and had 4 foster children all ages 4 and 5. She was like a drill sergeant. Her kids had the same bedtime, same dinnertime, same playtime and same time to do chores every day. She never wavered and the children would never get snacks or something they wanted unless they followed her rules. If they didn't, it was a time out, no questions asked. She was very firm, but very fair. The kids loved her and respected her. These kids all had parents who were drug addicts and generally terrible parents, but they were very happy with this foster mother because the children had discipline, consistency and positive reinforcement.
4. Don't argue with the children or even negotiate anything that may get them off schedule. Kids loves boundaries, schedules and consistency. You'll notice most grade school teachers are good at these things and the best teachers are very good and extremely predictable. Teachers may have 20 – 30 kids and they cannot afford to be inconsistent or allow any student to be disruptive. Disruption is bad for the kids, the teacher and the individual students.

5. Nutrition is very important for children. When I worked with kids at different schools, I noticed most kids and most schools were serving and eating junk food. Teachers will often use candy or sugary snacks to entice children or reward them. Unfortunately, when the kids go home, they crash and have trouble sleeping at night. Use the smoothie recipe in this book and cut the amount in half, but it's a great way to start the day and gives them all the nutrition they need to concentrate better.

6. Grounding is now used in many schools around the country. Go to grounded.com and watch the movie. Teachers will explain how it works and the tremendous results they are seeing. You can buy a grounding mat on Amazon for about $30. They're very safe and they have been proven effective with children's behavior at school. You can certainly use it at home or for sleep as well.

7. Parents involved in their children's education is extremely important. Behavior and grades are often linked to the interaction with children and their parents. Be involved, help the kids when possible and always recognize school work and reinforce any achievements. I did this with my kids and 35 years later I couldn't be closer to them. Your interaction during the school years will often set a precedent for your relationship with them for the rest of your life.

8. Adolescence can be a trying and difficult time, as your child is faced with the complexities of relationships, stress, possibly a job, self-esteem is a major concern, hormonal changes and the pressure of transitioning from childhood to adulthood. They need patience and support. A good place to start is a Vocational Aptitude Test, usually on-line, to identify strengths and areas your child may find interesting or is suited for. I took a test in the Air Force called ASVAB and it said radio and television broadcaster, which became my first career. I couldn't be happier, but in my mid-twenties, I had the

GI bill from the service that paid for any college course I wanted to take so I took another vocational aptitude test and it said psychologist. I've never looked back. It is very reassuring to know what might work and it provides light at the end of the tunnel, something needed by most adolescents. The famous author Mark Twain once said, "My parents were such assholes when I was 16, but by the time I reached 18, I was amazed at how much they had learned in 2 years. Obviously, he had changed, grown out of adolescence and was becoming an adult. Adolescence can last much longer for some people. My son was stuck until he was 22 but at 35 today, he is a licensed nurse, happily married with 2 kids and is very well adjusted. Everybody's different.

9. Parenting can test a marriage like nothing else. The main problems are time and money. You've got to make family a priority and realize that almost everything else will take the back seat. Have friends with kids so you have something in common. Help each other out during this stressful time. The "Superwoman Complex" was first coined in the 70's when women were working, going to school, raising children and keeping a marriage. Everyone needs to practice stress management, practice good nutrition and have some way to release and downshift or you will be a prime candidate for illness or worse. Debt is the # 1 problem that results in divorce. You must follow a budget, get out of debt or at least get spending in control immediately. Buy used stuff and do with less. You have enough problems with kids and you don't need debt to make things worse. I guarantee you – you can't take anything with you to your grave site. Just drive through a junk yard sometime and look at all the stuff that people paid good money for and probably even financed. It's NOT worth it. Get out of debt and enjoy your family. There's nothing more important than your children.

10. Tough love is just that – it's love. Being a parent isn't easy. It may be the greatest thing you'll ever do. I would put my kids near the top of my list. Being a parent is a privilege and great joy, but it is difficult. Everything in life that's special: pregnancy, a college degree, parenting, retirement, earning social security, paying off your 30-year house mortgage. The best things in life are the hardest things and will require a lot from you, but they are so WORTH IT.

Chapter 18 – Alignment in the Workplace

Most of us spend about 1/3 of our lives in and around the workplace. It can be the best part of our lives or often times, the worst. Most people are living in the balcony or the basement. You have to decide what represents balcony for you. You only need 1 job and 1 career and you only need to pay your bills. Until you get your spending under control, you may be setting yourself up for failure. You're just working to pay off the bills, which is often the first step or motivating factor that keeps you in the basement.

I strongly believe in vocational aptitude tests and I mentioned in an earlier chapter that it is a good thing for teenagers to do so they can have light at the end of the tunnel. Vocational aptitude tests are available on line and some colleges and libraries have them. The military uses a vocational aptitude test called the ASVAB. This test absolutely nailed me and helped me get started when I was 17 years old. I have seen so many kids when I was practicing that were lost and lacked focus which ultimately affected their self-esteem and caused them to make bad decisions, such as drugs and alcohol and some even chose criminal behavior. Young people need direction, but even middle age people can feel lost and confused so it's not a bad thing to take a vocational aptitude test even at an advanced age to ensure that you are on the right course or the test results may give you some ideas that will help you get unstuck.

Sometimes your way isn't working and your job can be difficult to endure. You may feel overwhelmed and below are 3 reasons why your job may not be working for you.

Pride – You don't want anybody to think you can't handle it so you avoid or cover it up. Sometimes, the lie is worse than the original problem. You want people at work to think you're in charge and you've got it all together. You think you can handle everything yourself, even If you have to work extra hours to cover your weaknesses or faults.

Fear – You can't admit you tried as hard as you could, but came up empty. You are afraid people will think less of you. You're afraid to listen and do the right thing because you may have to go a direction you don't feel comfortable with.

Stubbornness – You're unwilling to change the way you do things. "It's my way or the highway." Sometimes the greatest enemy of tomorrow's success is yesterday's success.

Basement people are often stuck and afraid, unwilling to change, surrendering to doing it "the way it's always worked in the past" and choosing to follow the leader instead of being in touch with what's important to them. A good thing to do is consider what's really important with any job. National statistics from experts say that job satisfaction is the most important thing to most people. Money is #6 on the list. We all have to earn enough money, but if you live within a budget, buy second hand stuff at Goodwill, thrift shops, garage sales and e-bay you would be surprised at how much money you can save and that takes pressure off getting more money at work. Debt is a 4-letter word and the reason for most divorces. Don't let it be a reason for job dissatisfaction. Get out of debt as soon as possible. I often referred my clients to lexingtonlaw.com and they got help getting out of debt and raised their credit score so they could buy a house or car. Debt and poor financial management will keep you in the basement and may affect marriage, jobs or relationships, especially if you have children.

Knowing when to move on is a fine art. Job stability isn't what it used to be many years ago. My father worked for General Motors for 35 years and then he died. That was a very common practice with his generation, but today people move a lot and change jobs often compared to 60 years ago. Working for a company for 30 years and getting a gold watch and a pension are almost gone. That is exactly what my father was given by General Motors, but unfortunately, he didn't have any time or good health to enjoy either.

Today, pension plans have been replaced by 401 K plans which can be lucrative if you invest wisely. The key to success in the stock market is to pick a few good stocks and properly diversify, not diworseify. Most people pick stocks they like or try to get rich quick so they are really gambling instead of investing. Pick a great stock portfolio manager. I personally limit my stock portfolio to about 4 stocks and all of them I carefully scrutinize frequently. Remember, the stock market can be a roller coaster ride and you have to trust your advisor and be patient. A long-term approach is best and patience is a virtue. Most rich people will invest in real estate or the stock market. Do your homework, associate with people whom you trust (who know what they are doing) and be careful, trust is earned, so find talented people who will help you. Profit and success are rarely easy or quick. It takes hard work, good advice from people you trust and patience.

The formula for success in business is to align with the following:

a. Reduce Fear – Always prepare yourself for the worse. This isn't being negative; it's just being realistic. Businesses can close, bosses can leave, the economy can sour....so many things can go wrong. Stability is great, but have a backup plan. You will feel more secure and comfortable.

b. Manage your finances - It's not how much you make; it's how much you spend. Buy second hand at thrift shops. Stick to the budget and save whatever you can. Jobs and marriages can fall apart when there is financial tension.

c. Don't be insane – Insanity is doing the same thing over and over and expecting different results. You've got to be flexible and roll with the punches.

d. Avoid the Boss spelled backwards (Double SOB) – Unfortunately we've all worked with SOB's and you may have had to live with them in some capacity. I had many SOB bosses in the military and I never got creative or tried to figure them out. I just said "Yes Sir" or "No Sir" and told myself "This too shall pass." It feels like forever but it never lasts that long and sometimes we have to put up with short term pain for long term gain. Always have a backup plan as well because the SOB can just be too much sometimes.

e. I have spotted the enemy and the enemy is me – We can be our own worst enemy. I know I've had to get out of my way several times. The old saying is that I would never join a club that would accept me as a member. It's hard to be humble, but in this age of narcissism it's a good trait to learn because almost no one wants to work with a self-centered asshole. You have to be flexible, humble and considerate. These are also traits that happen to work well in a marriage. Both marriage and job success are about getting along with other people. You have to be a "team player". I had to learn these traits and the most difficult part was I didn't realize it until I was told. I thought I was a pretty good guy, but I learned that many people saw some flaws I didn't see. The other problem is denial. You really don't want to accept those traits, but if it is true, my advice is to accept the truth, swallow your pride, learn humility and be grateful for every little thing you have. An attitude of gratitude is the healthiest emotion you can have and will really help with relationships and the work place.

Alignment In the workplace can be the most difficult alignment because you may not like the people you work with and are forced to so you can survive, sometimes for much longer than you planned because you need the money or this is the best that you can do currently. This story is not often seen in movies, but it is often reality and becomes the main reason that leads to divorce, illness, financial problems and depression. You have to stop and assess your situation and prove to yourself you're doing the right thing. Go to the career center and be sure there are no other jobs or employment situations. I have been to my local career center several times in my lifetime because I felt at the time, I needed a backup and an alternative. Trust me, there always is. Remember, there are only 3 things that matter in life: relationships, health and financial security. The less you spend and the more you save, the better you feel. Take good care of yourself. Don't eat junk and try intermittent fasting when you can to get healthy and save money. Try the smoothie mentioned in this book to give you more energy and keep you healthy. Spend less on restaurant food and stay home more if you need to. Financial health is extremely important. Remember, God specializes in the impossible. Prayer and asking for help are a great idea. My entire life has been helped by prayer and so many wonderful things happened to me that I simply cannot explain.

What do you need and what do you want? More than likely, you have been worrying about things you want or you have been wasting time and money on things you don't really need. Go to the local junkyard and look at all the cars, furniture and clothes that so many people spent a fortune on, especially things they financed. Go to a third world country as I have. You make so much more than their citizens but we spend so much more. We don't save, but some countries have people averaging 25% per year savings. Americans often choose debt.

Alignment at work can depend on how well you manage your checkbook. You can't expect your mate to throw you a life preserver when you are drowning in debt. You decided to swim in the deep water and you will discover that you have to swim back to the safe, shallow water. Would you want to be your mate? Is it hard living with you? Are you considerate and caring or are you so wrapped up in your world and not focused on anyone else? Losing at solitaire is something I understand. Other people want to help you, if you let them. Your job is important, but other people in your life are more important. Stop and smell the roses. Don't fly solo and let the people who care about you help. Sometimes you just need someone to listen to you.

Follow these steps when you feel lost, overwhelmed or extremely frustrated:

1 – Make sure you align physically – ground, intermittent fasting, eat organic food, drink the smoothie listed in this book, exercise (the best exercise is the one you'll do), sleep well (Casper is a great affordable mattress, if you need a new one), hydrate (at least 64 ounces of water daily)

2 – Eliminate or reduce financial stress - set a budget, get out of debt, buy good used stuff

3 – Journal your feelings – a great way to express your feelings and you can go back in your journal to see how you've worked things out or are improving. If work stress persists, your journal is a safe place to vent your feelings and may be telling you to go look for a new job.

4 – Don't speak to anyone at work. No one can keep a secret, especially juicy work gossip. You never have to worry about gossip if you never tell anyone. Journal your thoughts and feelings and tell someone you trust who is far removed from your job. You need to tell someone, but make sure it's not someone at work.

5 – Always go to the career center to see what's available and also register on indeed.com to find new work

6 – Take a vocational aptitude test to help you clarify what you would be best at.

Moving from the basement to the balcony requires focus, alignment and commitment. Sometimes sacrifices are necessary and realizing what you were made to be by your creator is extremely important and will help you achieve real prosperity. I have worn many hats during my lifetime and the experiences prepared me for writing this book and living God's purpose for me. I am in my element and when I balance my checkbook and take care of my health, I feel amazing. Helping you is very rewarding and I am doing what I was created to do. Life is so much easier and so much better! Life in the balcony is what you were created for. I hope you find the courage and discipline to live in the balcony!

Chapter 19 – The 40 Day Treatment Plan

It took a lifetime to get where you are today. So many unfulfilled dreams, disappointments, victories and losses. It's how you became you today. Take the time to scale from 0 – 100 your self-esteem, frustration tolerance, Impulse control and mood. Don't worry if you start low. My clients averaged 20 of 100, but by the time you successfully complete this treatment plan you will score much higher. Work on each subject below daily, journal your experiences and go back to your journal when done to measure and understand your progress.

Day 1 – Love and Accept Yourself Unconditionally (LOVE IS A VERB)

Day 2 – Buy and Use a Grounding Pad (try Amazon)

Day 3 – Let Go and Let God (trust God)

Day 4 – Make a List of Past Problems and Forgive Yourself and Everyone Who Hurt You

Day 5 – Drink the Smoothie Daily

Day 6 – STOP eating SUGAR! It is the main cause of most diseases today!

Day 7 – Buy an Ionic Water Shower (Amazon - $20)

Day 8 – Try intermittent fasting

Day 9 – Eat Organic Food – Try Amy's Organic Frozen Foods, Chili and Soups – Walmart

Day 10 – Row, Walk or Exercise Daily

Day 11 – Start a date night with your companion. (Alternate events)

Day 12 – Take 250 mg Daily Chelated Magnesium at night (add melatonin for insomnia)

Day 13 – You Will Attract What You Radiate (focus on positive energy)

Day 14 – Drink alkaline water daily (from your ionic shower is good)

Day 15 – Don't Have the Eyesight of an Eagle and the Vision of a Clam (make healthy decisions)

Day 16 – Don't Fertilize Forty Acre Fields with Farts (finish and adequately complete)

Day 17 – Live in Faith Not in Fear

Day 18 – Love is a Verb – an action word (not a person, place or thing – noun)

Day 19 – Have an Attitude of Gratitude (Be grateful for everything)

Day 20 – Love is not to be Found, but to be Made

Day 21 – Debt is a 4-Letter Word (avoid and retire debt when possible)

Day 22 – Develop an Honest Budget and Stick to It!

Day 23 – The Body is a Temple – Focus from the Neck Down

Day 24 –Become a Second-Hand Millionaire (buy great used stuff)

Day 25 – Learn to tithe (check out Malachi 3:10)

Day 26 – Save money regularly (no matter how small)

Day 27 – Learn to be a Giver (until it hurts so good)

Day 28 – Don't Resist it Replace it (all addictions)

Day 29 – Learn to Be Considerate

Day 30 – Reduce and Eliminate Frustration (anger management)

Day 31 – Eliminate Impulsiveness (#1 reason for addiction)

Day 32 – Improve Self-Esteem (scale first – know what you need)

Day 33 – Stop Seeking Approval (love and accept yourself)

Day 34 – Reduce Selfish Pride (be humble)

Day 35 – Eliminate the Musts and Shoulds in Your Life

Day 36 – Resign from living for NEXT and MORE

Day 37 – Understand and Incorporate Discipline

Day 38 – Be Humble, Considerate and Grateful

Day 39 – Unconditionally Love and Accept Yourself

Day 40 – Listen to Daily Hope podcast (pastorrickwarren. com)

This 40-day plan will lead you back to who you were meant to be. You will eliminate all the elements that have led you away from the person you are. Accept yourself and love yourself. There's only one of you in the entire universe. You're an original not a copy!

Chapter 20 – Alignment with God

The first task in aligning with God is deciding if a God really exists. After viewing progress first hand from thousands of clients over 30 years, the absolute wonders of nutrition, the capabilities of the human body and when I consider the awe and beauty of nature, I firmly believe there is a Creator and we are children of God. You are completely unique. No one else in the Universe has your finger prints, thumb prints, eye prints and voice print. You are one of a kind. There must be a Creator!

After answering the question of God for yourself, a good next step is to decide if there are any answers religion provides. The Case for Christ is a book and movie that highlights the nearly 2 -year research project of an atheist whose wife had just converted to Christianity and explores if it has merit. The thesis of this project was that Christ was resurrected after 3 days and over 500 eyewitnesses saw him when he came back to earth. Several different enemies also saw him and verified that he came back from death. The book and movie highlight the author's journey exploring the archaeological findings from a PhD, psychological ramifications from the American Psychological Association and medical issues from the American Medical Association. In all, he spoke with 13 different doctors and experts and after almost 2 years of research this investigator, who has a law degree from Yale University and is a nationally published author, also cited that many eyewitnesses saw Christ during the 40 days he was on earth after his resurrection. As hard as he tried, he could not prove that Christianity was a hoax and he realized time was divided between B.C. (before Christ) and AD (anno domini – the Year of our Lord) for a very good reason. Christianity was real. He became a Christian. The author's son and daughter became Christians (earned advanced degrees in Christianity) and many years later he has written several books about Christianity and has a wide following on You Tube. He teaches at a Christian College in Texas. His name is Lee Stroebel.

After you've answered the questions of a Creator and Savior then you have to decide if the Bible is a good blueprint for living. I can tell you after receiving 3 college degrees, attending numerous seminars and 30 years of practice, nothing comes close to the Bible. The best thing you can do is listen to the Daily Hope podcast from Pastor Rick Warren, PhD. everyday. You will learn so much about the greatest and best-selling book ever and how to incorporate it into your daily life. Absolutely everything you need to know about relationships, financial management, health and the afterlife are all there and will help you, far more than psychology or any other science can ever help.

A relationship with God is built on trust and faith. You have to let go and let God. You are a child of God and if you follow the advice of the Bible, you will be prosperous. Everything takes time and you have to be patient, but faith will get you to prosperity. The world is built on MORE and NEXT and is very temporary. You can't take all your possessions in a U-Haul to your grave site. All the stuff you work so hard for and want so bad is staying behind. You're only taking you with you and the most important characteristic is Love. The bible is built on love and there are so many examples of the heroes of the Bible who messed up so badly but were forgiven. Paul, who wrote most of the New Testament, was the greatest Christian who ever lived. Paul started life as Saul from Tarsus and was a Christian terrorist. He killed Christians for a living. Through grace from God described in Acts, he was converted and changed his name to Paul. He became the greatest example of Christian faith man has ever seen. He built the Christian church.

The process for having a great relationship with God is to focus on love, wellness and prosperity. Begin by accepting love is a verb, an action word and be humble, be considerate and be grateful to define your personality. Then align your love with other people. Love comes from God and is transmitted through you and will only flow when you are humble, considerate and grateful. You are a child of God and you need his help and grace to be the best you can be.

It can be difficult, but focus on your SHAPE (Spiritual Gifts, Heart, Abilities, Personality and Experiences) as a tool to discover the purpose God has for you. What are you good at? What do you like? I've always had success with writing in various capacities, but today I am surrendering to what I believe is my SHAPE and the purpose God created for me. I am in my element. I wish the same for you and no matter what sacrifice you make; God will always take the failures in your life and create victories when you are aligned with him.

Remember, your body is a temple and gift from God. First, you have to ground or be one with the earth. You are an inflammatory mess because you are not grounded. Adam and Eve were completely grounded and connected to the earth. Humans have not been grounded since the 50's because we wear artificial clothes, specifically tennis shoes, which insulates us from the earth. When you plug into a grounding pad, you are receiving the earth's free flowing electrons and the billions of free radicals floating around your body will be neutralized. They are missing an electron and when you supply electrons from the earth, you will be grounded and your health will improve.

You have to detoxify and rid your body of toxins that are causing cellular dysfunction. Our bodies begin to deteriorate by age 40, especially if you are eating the Standard American Diet (SAD). The importance of mitochondrial health is critical to cellular health. Aging is a process that is prompted by mitochondrial dysfunction driving cellular decline. There are three major mechanisms driving cellular decline and causes us to age and experience disease. The following three reasons describe the aging process. The smoothie mentioned in this book, grounding and fasting will help you manage the 3 problems with aging mentioned below.

1. A decline in mitochondrial health which reduces efficiency in cellular energy production.
2. A decline in NAD+ which impairs the natural process that turns nutrients into energy production.
3. A decline in glutathione which is the master antioxidant.
4. Fasting prompts the body to detoxify. It was awarded a Nobel Prize in 2016 because a Japanese professor proved autophagy or detoxification was a valid and key benefit of fasting. Most scientists today believe that autophagy or detoxification begins about 14 hours into a fast.

After grounding and fasting, nutrition is the next step to wellness. Organic food that is raw or prepared in temperatures below 116 degrees Fahrenheit will preserve the enzymes and be nutritious. It is easiest to mix raw organic foods in a blender for a smoothie and drink it every day. The smoothie mentioned in this book will give you everything you need. Add alkaline water combined with the smoothie and your pH will increase. Otto Warburg, MD won the Nobel prize when he proved that disease cannot thrive in an alkaline pH. Your blood is always slightly alkaline – about 7.3 pH, if you drink the smoothie and ionic alkaline water, you should raise your total body pH to about the same.

Just add exercise, walking and swimming are great. My favorite exercise is rowing. You will exercise about 90% of your muscles, and you get both cardiovascular benefits and resistance training. Rowing is something you can do at home so weather or inconvenience is never an issue.

When you are earthing or grounding, fasting, eating the right nutrition and exercising properly, you may experience better sleep, better energy, pain relief, improved blood flow and overall better health.

Prosperity is achieved by putting God first in your finances. The Bible recommends avoiding or retiring debt, living by a budget and appreciating what you have, tithing which helps you learn to give and help others and saving or investing which helps you get the things you need. It's always about trusting God and putting Him first in your finances, which is why I tithe before I do anything. He comes first. When you are grateful and trust God to help you, even when it seems impossible, that's when the miracles happen. Finding God's purpose is absolutely critical for long term success and happiness.

Many years ago, I was headed for bankruptcy, unable to work due to a stroke, recently divorced after a 26-year marriage with two kids and I had to lose 200 pounds. I was having a really bad day, but I had faith and just trusted God because I couldn't get out of the mess I had created. I had spotted the enemy and the enemy was me. Once you become humble, accept that you are a child of God and it's not about you, your life gets better. You have to trust God.

You are one of a kind – a work of art. You have unique fingerprints, unique thumbprints, unique eye prints and a unique voice print. There is no one else like you in the Universe. There are over 7 billion people on planet earth and no one, NO ONE else is like you. God threw away the mold when he made you. You are not a random creation of the universe. It is literally amazing that 7 billion people on this planet are completely unique. Every snowflake is completely unique. No 2 snowflakes are alike. No 2 people are alike. You are a masterpiece and there will never be another person like you. When you die, you will take your unique finger prints, thumb prints, eye prints, voice print and your DNA with you. You are special and when you realize how special you are and how much God loves you, you will feel free, accepted and loved. Maybe for the first time in your life. You will realize there is a home in heaven and you will understand that insanity on this planet often exists because we have free will and we make bad choices. The glass can be half full instead of half empty.

Alignment with God is surrendering and trusting your Creator. It's realizing that the only currency that matters is love, not money. Wellness is a gift and when you fast, ground, eat healthy foods and exercise, you begin to reap the rewards of the universe and feel and look terrific. Prosperity only comes from managing debt, tithing and saving. When you are aligned with God, it all comes together and when you trust Him, you will finally start living His purpose for you. It often doesn't happen overnight, but when it becomes a lifestyle, it will all come together in the most amazing ways!

Affirmations

Affirmations are a great way to combat stinking thinking and move your mind away from stressful thoughts. Affirmations are thoughts and ideas that could happen instead of focusing on the thoughts and events that have failed and brought you misery in the past. Life can be a glass that is either half full or half empty – your choice. Affirmations are a choice for a life that is half full and getting better. The following affirmations saved my life in 2008 and got me out of the basement and into the balcony. I hope they do the same for you.

1. I am radiating and attracting love and prosperity today.
2. I am achieving my highest good today.
3. Divine restoration is now taking place.
4. Only success will come into my life today.
5. I face the present and future wise, secure and unafraid.
6. I let go and forgive everyone who hurt me today.
7. I am letting go of my dead past and unborn future. I live in the now.
8. I am letting go of all barriers (grief, shame, abuse, abandonment, divorce, failure) and triggers (basement people, places and things). I live in the balcony today.
9. I am completely accepted, totally forgiven, secure and prosperous today.
10. Happiness is where I am.

Resources

1. *Debt Advice – lexingtonlaw.com*
2. *Investment Advice – Dave Ramsey. com, smartvestor.com*
3. *Relationships, Self Esteem – pastorrick.com (Daily Hope podcast)*
4. *Earthing, Grounding – grounded.com*
5. *Fasting - Dr. Mindy Pelz, True North Clinic, Dr. Valter Longo, USC, Jason Fung, M.D. (You Tube)*
6. *Wellness Research – pubmed.org*
7. *discoverthealignmentfocusedlife.com – My web site*

Top 20 Medical Tests

There are many medical tests that can be helpful, but the following 20 tests will give you a snapshot that will help you in your wellness journey. I always recommend consulting a licensed functional medical doctor to help you understand the results of the tests and assist you in your quest for good health.

1. Body Fat Percentage – below 19%
2. Blood Pressure – 120/80 or below
3. Total Cholesterol – Below 200 (150 is ideal)
4. LDL – 100 or less
5. HDL – 60 or above
6. LPA – 30 or less
7. Triglycerides – 100 or less
8. Vitamin D – 100
9. SED (inflammation) - 30 or below
10. C - reactive protein – 1 or 2
11. A1C Hemoglobin – 7.0 or below (blood sugar)
12. Homocysteine – 5 to 10
13. Blood Sugar – 80 – 100
14. pH – slightly above 7.0
15. DMSA (heavy metals) – detox mercury
16. Cortisol – 6 -23 mcg
17. Bowel Movements – 1 to 2 daily, (light brown, toothpaste texture)
18. BNP – 100 or less (heart)
19. Thyroid – 0.5 – 5.0 ml
20. Fiber – 25 grams daily

10 Reasons to Buy This Book Today

1. Learn How the Author Lost 200 Pounds and Kept it Off
2. Learn How the Author Rebounded from a Stroke and 5-month Coma
3. Learn Individual, Group, Family and Parenting Therapy from 30 Years of Practice
4. Learn Behavior Modification with Children
5. Learn Addictions Counseling – From the Neck Up
6. Learn Earthing – The Key to Pain Management, Depression and Insomnia Relief
7. Learn About Wellness – The Body is a Temple
8. Learn Financial Management – From Debt to Prosperity
9. Learn Stress Management – From Anxiety to Peace
10. Learn the Miracle of Autophagy – The Nobel Prize Winning Solution for Detoxification